AF334075

THE RICHES OF HIS GRACE

THE RICHES OF HIS GRACE

by

ROBERT MENZIES, D.D.

JAMES CLARKE & CO. LIMITED
33 STORE STREET, LONDON, W.C.1

TO

MY WIFE

without whose help and encouragement
this book would not have been written

First published 1956

Printed in Great Britain by
The Camelot Press Ltd., London and Southampton

CONTENTS

ACKNOWLEDGMENTS

I would like to acknowledge my indebtedness to Rev. A. S. Mair of Forres, for carefully revising the proofs, and to Rev. Ronald Wallace of Lanark, for some useful suggestions.

I

PROLOGUE: A GREAT MAN'S PROUD BOAST
(*For post-Easter*)

I am not ashamed of the Gospel. I see it as the very power of God working for the salvation of everyone who believes it, both Jew and Greek. I see in it God's plan for imparting righteousness to men, a process begun and continued by their faith (Rom. i. 16-17, J. B. Phillips).

PAUL'S way of stating his attitude to the gospel is worth observing. "I am not ashamed of the Gospel" he wrote, as if he were registering a protest against the current view. Some commentators suggest that here Paul was merely indulging in a figure of speech, known as litotes, which consists in understating the situation in order to throw into relief its importance. This is unlikely to be the case. Most probably he speaks of shame in connection with the gospel because that was the feeling generally attached to it. He is merely reflecting the reaction of the natural man to the claims of the gospel. In certain of its external features at least there were reasons for this sense of shame. Its Founder was a Jew, a member of a despised race. He was moreover an inconspicuous Jew of no social or political status, merely a peasant, brought up in one of the obscurest and most despised provinces of the Roman Empire, and one who earned His bread in the sweat of His brow. At the end of His earthly career Rome impaled Him on a cross between two malefactors. To these derogatory circumstances must be added the offence that that shameful cross was made the corner stone in the edifice of the new gospel. To the righteous Jew that Cross was a scandal, to the enlightened Greek it was foolishness, but to the haughty Roman it was revolting. Cicero, commenting on the sadistic nature of this instrument of torture of Rome's devising, added, "it should never even be mentioned in connection with the sacred person of a Roman citizen."

It is against that background of general despisal that we must measure the audacity of Paul's claim for the gospel. The unregenerate world might feel a sense of shame, if asked to espouse this gospel; but as for himself, no such feeling was present. On the contrary, he was so consumed with the love of this gospel and his sense of its intrinsic worth that he was ready and eager to preach it to those that were in Rome also. In our text he gives his reasons for this legitimate pride. What he has to say is merely a brief and naked summary of his case for the gospel but even in this minimal form his apologetic is so challengingly provocative and so richly suggestive that it deserves closer scrutiny.

First of all Paul is not ashamed of the gospel *because it is clothed with divine power*. It had its source in God and not in any decree of Caesar, and having the grace and love of God beating at the heart of it it produced supernatural results. In the background of Paul's mind there existed the glaring contrast between this type of power and that other type which Rome so strikingly represented. For Rome also was the symbol of power, the power of a vast secular civilisation. Seated on her seven hills this proud city exercised an authority which extended to the farthest reaches of the then known world. She was the seat of the world's government, the source of her enlightened legal system, the home of the arts, the centre of culture, the emporium of the world's commerce, the dumping-ground for all the religions which came from the East. From Rome radiated the great highways along which the legions ceaselessly marched to hold together in peace the outposts of her vast Empire. She was a mighty Colossus, representing material power in its most impressive form. But alas, she was destitute of the moral constraints which could make and keep her life wholesome. Her ancient pieties had crumbled. Her inner life was corrupt. Master of the world, she had lost the secret of mastering herself. She had gained the whole world and lost her soul. Paul was eager to preach the gospel to those in Rome because he knew he possessed in his gospel the only power that could meet this need.

A ministerial friend of mine was on one occasion showing his son a high-powered locomotive recently built. "Just think, Donald," he said, "that engine cost as much to build as our Church did." "Yes," said the boy brightly, "but then, Dad, *it goes*!" Paul was proud of the gospel because it was a going concern. In his own experience he had made full proof of it. It had wrought mightily in himself. It had apprehended him on the road to Damascus, and turned him from being a persecuting fanatic into an ardent Apostle. It needed great power to effect that change. As a missionary he was deeply conscious of the Gospel's wonder-working power. He had tried it out in great centres of pollution, Antioch in Syria, Ephesus in Asia Minor, Corinth in Greece; and everywhere it worked. His testimony was that "the weapons of our warfare are mighty before God for the demolishing of fortresses" of evil. He was confident that the results it had hitherto achieved would be reproduced in Rome.

This is still the ground of our pride in the gospel. It is still the power of God unto salvation. When we make use of the gospel we are handling the levers of power. The Cross is still what Paul said it was, not only "the wisdom" but "the power of God". The Resurrection of Jesus is the supreme demonstration of the power of God. His holy Spirit shed abroad in the hearts of all believers is the spirit of power. And the exceeding greatness of the power that worketh in us mightily is, as Paul writes in Ephesians, "the same energy which was demonstrated in Christ, when God raised Him from the dead, and gave Him the place of supreme honour in Heaven." All these forces inherent in the gospel are still available for our use, and are still bringing forth their perfect fruit in transfigured lives. When we remember that man's chronic condition is one of moral inability, and that we possess in this gospel the one and only means of redressing this tragic situation, have we any reason to be ashamed of it?

More specifically and as a particular application of our last thought Paul is not ashamed of the gospel *because of its power to set right what is wrong in all our personal relationships.* "For therein" writes Paul (A.V.) "is revealed the righteousness of God from faith to faith" an admittedly obscure translation. J. B. Phillips more clearly renders, "I see in it God's plan for imparting righteousness to men, a process begun and continued by their faith." Roughly what the passage means is that the gospel is God's way of setting right what is at present wrong in our personal relations, and that this plan is based on faith from start to finish. Paul's explanatory addendum "the just shall live by faith" might be more clearly translated, as Wm. Barclay does, "It is the man who is in a right relationship with God as a result of his faith who really lives." Here then in this passage and in the verses which follow is a revelation of the human plight the gospel is designed to meet. Paul's fundamental postulate is that unredeemed human nature is in a state of lostness. It has lost its way to the knowledge of the true and living God. Had it been concerned to know the way, the light of Nature would have served as guide, but even that light they had turned into darkness. In place of worshipping the true God they practised the grossest forms of idolatry. Wrong at the centre, they were wrong everywhere else. With the decay of true religion went the collapse of morals. The sacred use of sex was prostituted to the most revolting and unnatural purposes amongst both men and women. Thirteen out of fourteen Roman Emperors were homosexualists. Concurrently with this sexual perversity went the darkening of the mind, the corruption of the heart and sclerosis of the conscience. In verses 29–32 of this chapter Paul gives a fearsome list of the anti-social vices which ravaged the Roman society of his day, and we have no reason to suppose that the list was exhaustive. The nadir of degradation was reached when they are charged by Paul with not only glorying in their shame but inciting others to indulge in the same shamelessness.

Paul is often charged with painting too black a picture of the morals of the Roman society of his day, but the fact is that he greatly understates the truth. Contemporary Roman historians and moralists go far beyond Paul in their impeachment of Roman morals. They represent the period as an age of shame, a God-defying and a God-abandoned age, an age of voluptuousness, luxury, pleasure, cruelty and unnatural vices which seemed to be beyond any remedy. Rome needed desperately to be set right, if it were not to perish of internal decay. And that was why Paul was eager to preach the gospel to those that were in Rome. He believed that his gospel possessed a cleansing virtue that could arrest Rome's moral decay and rejuvenate its spiritual life at the source. That was another of the reasons why he was not ashamed of the gospel of Christ.

A gospel that can work a miracle of this nature is worth believing and trusting. That is why we are proud of it now and continue to commend it to all alike. The need for such a gospel is still clamant. To be sure, modern civilisation is not as far sunk as Rome's was. The Christian leaven has not wrought in vain. Yet the shadow of shame still darkly falls across the modern scene. No special Christian revelation is necessary to remind us that there is much that is wrong in our personal and national life, and that needs to be set right. Nearly all the vices Paul lists in this chapter could any day be paralleled from the columns of the daily newspaper. There is something radically and desperately wrong with our modern world. It is involved in a network of personal and corporate sin from which it seems powerless to extricate itself. "No visitor from another planet," writes Herbert Farmer, "having seen our slums, vice, mental and bodily diseases and breakdowns, our social and industrial systems, and the culmination of it all in the threat of atomic war, could do any other than go back and report that something, Heaven knows what, is desperately wrong with the race of earth-dwellers."

Such being our tragic human plight it is clear that no

salvation is to be found along humanistic lines. Long ago Epictetus, noting the need, hinted also at the remedy. "We need a hand let down from Heaven to lift us up." For we cannot lift ourselves up. All modern substitutes for the gospel—education, social planning, legislation, scientific techniques, mental healing and the like—fail to touch the root of our disease. Only God, working mightily for us and in us through His gospel can meet our case. That is why we, like Paul, are proud of the gospel. It is God's plan for rectifying these maladjustments which have the effect of darkening our knowledge of God, of splitting up the unity of our nature, and poisoning our relations with our fellow-beings.

A third reason why Paul was not ashamed of the Gospel *was concerned with its method of working*. It was a process that rested on faith from start to finish. It began its regenerating work in the believer's heart by an initial act of trust in the finished work of the Redeemer. It continued its gracious work by repeated acts of self-committal to the same Saviour. And there was no point in the whole saving process where men could dispense with reliance on Christ. Men only lived a life of grace as they stood in this dependent relationship to Christ. That is the gospel's method of working. It depends on faith from start to finish.

Now this may seem to us a familiar and even commonplace thing to say, but in reality it is probably the most original and revolutionary conception that has ever dawned on the mind of man. This discovery is more significant for the welfare of mankind than Galileo's discovery that the earth revolved round the sun, or Darwin's *Origin of Species*, or Rutherford's fission of the atom. For see what it means. It shifted the whole pivot of salvation from man to God. It makes the hope of the world to depend, not on man's futile ability to solve the human dilemma, but on the mighty power of God. This was quite a new approach to the problem of salvation. The great universal religions of the world are all autosoteric in that they rely for their effect on man alone. Nearly all the modern schemes also for redressing what is wrong in life rest on human volition. This is the great fallacy which underlies modern scientific humanism and Communism. All alike, spite of experience to the contrary, continue to cling to the idea, that man, by his inventive skill, by his foresight and wisdom, by his exploitation of Nature's resources can achieve salvation. This fallacy lies at the root of modern pessimism. Paul in his pre-Christian days was of the same mind. And it was his disenchantment with the Jewish legal method which finally led him to his great discovery which has revolutionised men's thought about the whole problem of salvation. He discovered that what law could not do, what no human effort could do, could yet be successfully done, if men turned to God, committed themselves wholly to Him in an act of unconditional trust, and allowed Him to undertake for them the whole work of salvation. This is the secret of the glowing optimism that beats at the heart of the gospel. Things may be as awry and out of joint here to-day as they were in Rome long ago, but they are not hopeless when our great Deliverer is with us on the field of action. We can work out our own salvation hopefully when it is God that worketh in us both to will and do of His good pleasure. To the question "Who shall deliver me from this body of death?" we can, like Paul, hopefully reply, "God will. Thanks be to Him, through Jesus Christ our Lord."

A fourth reason why Paul was not ashamed of the gospel was *because of its range of reference, the width of its application.* One of the most glittering jewels on the Gospel's crown is the universality of its appeal. It was a gospel for everybody who fulfilled the one condition of trust in God as revealed in Christ. It was the saving power of God to *everyone* who believed. This all-inclusive nature of the gospel separates it from every other type of religion, and lends to it a glory all its own. In the Graeco-Roman civilisation of Paul's day there were many religions in vogue, but they only worked, when they worked at all, in special circumstances and under special conditions. The Jewish faith had a wide popularity in the ancient Roman world, but anyone who wished to benefit from it had first to be circumcised or, if a "God-fearer", observe the ordinances of the Jewish law. That limited the number of its adherents. In Greece they offered redemption to sin-sick souls, but to receive its benefits the enquirer was required to go to Eleusis or some other religious centre, go through initiatory rites, and undergo a painful process of purgation. In Rome the Stoics offered salvation to anxious weary souls but before their system worked it was necessary to be "enlightened" and become philosophers. And that was quite beyond the reach of simple people. Modern alternatives to the gospel are open to the same charge. The Gospel of Christ alone has no such limiting condition attached to it. It is the gospel for everybody, male or female, bond or free, high-born, low, rich or poor, Jew or Gentile. It is the broad democratic highway where men of every race and tongue and tribe may meet on the basis of a simple trust in God which is open to all, and down which they may march together till they pass through the golden gates of the city of God.

Here then is contained Paul's apologetic for what he elsewhere calls "the glorious gospel of the blessed God." Let us summarise his main points. He is proud of the gospel because it is divine in its origin, the embodiment of moral and spiritual power, efficacious in its results, unique in its technique, universal in the scope of its reference. Possessing such a gospel to-day have we any right to be ashamed of it? There are plenty of things we might well be ashamed of—our moral weakness and failure, our shoddy and shabby natures, our foolish pride and self-ishness, our resistance to the gospel, our neglect of it and our tolerance of these conditions which make the gospel necessary. But ashamed of a gospel that sets right all that is most wrong in the heart of man and society! A thousand times No. It is the one thing that is worthy of our boasting. Never apologise for the gospel. Accept it gratefully and trust in it fully. Lean all your weight on it for life and death. Appropriate its riches, and exploit its resources. Rejoice in it as one who finds great spoil. Commend it to others and propagate it to the ends of the earth. Let it, in you and through you have free course and be glorified. Make this your boast as it was once a great man's proud boast "I am not ashamed of the gospel. I see it as the very power of God working for the salvation of every one who believes it, both Jew and Greek. I see in it God's plan for imparting righteousness to men, a process begun and continued by their faith."

II

SOME FALSE HUMAN REACTIONS

1. We Grow Lukewarm

So, because you are lukewarm, neither hot nor cold, I am going to spit you out of my mouth (Rev. iii. 16, Moffatt).

OF all the seven Churches which witnessed to the truth of the Christian revelation in Asia Minor, the one which comes nearest to us to-day is unquestionably the ancient Church of Laodicea. It was a city Church. Its members were composed largely of merchants who had grown wealthy in the prosecution of the dye industry. It possessed the prestige which wealth, social influence, and security, carry with them. Yet, with all its unrivalled advantages, the verdict passed on its witness by this writer was failure. Indeed it was the most conspicuous failure of all the seven Churches. It is true that its life was immune from the grosser excesses that stained some of the other Churches. Yet it lacked the one thing needful, which the other Churches in some degree retained. It had lost its first love. It had allowed its spiritual passion to cool. It had grown lukewarm.

This tepid reaction to the challenge of the gospel is something we should seriously ponder; for it searches all our hearts. It is this Laodicean spirit which taints the life and witness of many modern Christians, and robs them of vitality and power. The sacred writer castigates this spirit of lukewarmness, because it is a featureless compromise, perilously poised between two extremes of feeling. It is a state that is neither cold nor hot, merely cool; that was not even warm, but just lukewarm. As he was addressing Christians who had once been baptised with the Holy Ghost and with fire, it represented a grave spiritual declension. It meant, not that the sacred fire was beginning to kindle and glow, but that its flame was languishing and dying. Soon it would fail and cease and disappear. This is so serious a condition of things that it merits our most anxious concern.

The causes of lukewarmness are many and complex. A certain weight must be attached to the influence of environment, to the prevailing dimness of faith, to the spiritual uncertainty of our modern age, to the gravitating power of secularism, and the pull of anti-Christian forces. "It is difficult to think well of God," said Madame de Sévigné, "when one hears Him everywhere spoken against." When the chariots of God drag heavily, those who find the going hard are apt to lose heart in their job. Yet we must be careful not to exaggerate the influence of environment, for more usually our spiritual torpor springs from some debility within rather than from the action of external forces. It is something that happens in us rather than to us which accounts for the waning of our zeal. The sacred writer in this connection specifies the invasion of the spirit of worldliness into the heart as the decisive factor in a declining faith. "I am rich. I am well off. I lack nothing." When gold becomes men's God, whether they are rich or poor, there is little room in the heart for the wealth which Christ alone supplies. On the other hand, it ought to be recognised that our Saviour in a different connection cited the cares which the lack of money brings with it as a factor equal in importance to the deceitfulness of riches in choking the good seed of the Word. But if it is neither of these reasons, perhaps it is some chronic and unconfessed sin, which is exhausting the oxygen which feeds the flame of the devotional life. Or perhaps it is a life grown lazy and inert in the Master's service, an unexercised faith which has become dulled through lack of the stimulus which resistance and challenge provoke. Or again, it may be due simply to carelessness and negligence in the use of the means of grace. We are all apt to forget that the fire on the altar needs constant feeding and tending. And if we grow remiss in the exercise of

prayer, or public worship, or Bible study, or the practice
of spiritual discipline, how can we maintain the spiritual
glow? Under such circumstances, how can we avoid being
anything else than lukewarm? We would be well advised,
in tracking our disease to its roots, to look for the source of
our trouble, not in circumstances, but in ourselves, in
some illicit influences in ourselves which are dislodging
Christ from the centre of our affections. "I counsel thee,"
says this writer, "to buy of me eye-salve that thou mayest
see."

One is impressed with the heavy inertia of lukewarmness. It is not a going concern. It lacks driving force and
momentum. It achieves no results. It lacks propulsive
power. "It profiteth nothing." It is valueless to the
individual. It is worse than useless for the culture and
enrichment of the religious life. It inevitably gravitates to
stagnation and sterility. "You are a miserable creature,"
says this writer of the lukewarm, "pitiful, poor, blind,
naked." To such meagre proportions does this lack-
lustre spirit dwarf the soul. And there is no profit in it for
others either. A colourless religious life influences and
inflames no one. A lukewarm faith is powerless to reproduce itself. It exercises no convincing nor converting
ministry.

Every Laodicean Church is a dwindling and dying
concern, without any hope of growth or expansion. It is
the bush that burns and is not consumed which provokes
the spirit of investigation. It is enthusiasm and not lukewarmness which makes converts. "One loving heart,"
said Augustine, "sets another on fire."

Chiefly however its impotence is seen in its complete
failure to meet contemporary need. One of the marks
which distinguish man from the animal creation is his
capacity for enthusiasm. In the pursuit of his secular aims
and ambitions man is not lukewarm. The sportsman goes
crazy over golf, cricket or tennis. The thorough-going
scientist gives himself wholly up to the prosecution of his
studies. And the business man scorns delights and lives
laborious days to make a success of his business. Nor is

Satan lukewarm in his consecration to vile ends. "The Devil," said Bishop Latimer, "is the diligentest bishop in all the parish." Evil has taken the field to-day like an army on the offensive. The world, the flesh, and the Devil are avid of conquest. The forces of secularism are enthusiastic in the advocacy of their claims. Communism makes of its ideology an exclusive religion. In a life and death struggle with a full-blooded and insolent paganism, where is the hope of success in holding to a faint and languishing faith? We are convinced that there are resources in the living Christ that can put all His enemies under His feet. But to command success these resources must be energetically brought into action, and exploited to the full. As "we wrestle, not against flesh and blood, but against spiritual wickedness in high places," so we must "take to ourselves the whole armour of God" if we are to resist the wiles of the Devil. A totalitarian paganism must be matched and countered by a totalitarian Christianity. A burning and crusading faith is the only type of religion that will prove itself equal to the demands of this iron age. A lukewarm faith will be swept like chaff before the rising wind.

Consider again how serious is the affront that such a lukewarm faith offers to the challenge of Christ's life and witness. What part or lot has Jesus Christ in this dull and lack-lustre spirit of indifference? Is there any trace of half-heartedness in Him? Words once applied to Dr. Thomas Chalmers can on a kinglier level be justly applied to Him. "His religion was a certain fiery thing which required and got the very flower and vigour of the spirit, the strength and sinews of the soul, the prime and top of the affections." There was a certain hot urge and imperious vehemence in His spirit which on more than one occasion amazed and startled His disciples. It is on record that His blood relations were so alarmed at His reckless impetuosity that they said, "He is beside Himself." And His enemies, marking the eager thrust of His indomitable purpose, attributed His divine ecstasy to demonic possession. "He hath a Devil," they said, "and is mad." He Himself claimed that His mission was to set the earth on fire, and His supreme sorrow was that the fire was so slow to kindle. On Gethsemane and on the Cross He endured the utterest contradiction of sinners, that He might demonstrate the completeness of His self-giving to the task of men's salvation.

Such being the temper of Christ's nature, it is difficult to conceive of any state of feeling more antipathetic to His own than one of cool and calculating unconcern. If men can look on the passion of Christ's life and death without any kindling of feeling, if the response to One who came not in water only but in blood be merely a bloodless one, a flabby and washy approval, a flat and flaccid emotion, then they are beyond the pale indeed. There is something revolting about such a worthless emotional reaction. Christ Himself felt it to be an insult. Opposition He could respect. Weakness He could condone. Misdirected enthusiasm He could use. Laodiceanism alone He scornfully repudiated. Sir John Seely says that the only classes of people in the Gospels for whom Christ reserved unmeasured condemnation were the insincere and the unenthusiastic. For hot-blooded people whose passions swept them off their feet He could and did make generous allowance. For those who made mistakes He offered forgiveness. For wandering prodigals, returning home all scarlet with their sins He gave the kiss of welcome. But the lukewarm His soul with loathing rejects. Hot water is stimulating; cold water is refreshing, but tepid water is nauseating. "So because you are lukewarm, neither cold nor hot, I am going to spit you out of my mouth."

Our treatment of this vice would be incomplete, if we did not add a word about its cure. This disease is much more easy to diagnose than to treat. One of the initial difficulties we encounter is the self-complacency of its victims. "I am quite interested in God, you know," remarked a young woman in one of the services, "but I can't say I am 'nuts' on Him." The lukewarm are apt to pride themselves on what they call their moderation, and affect to despise the extravagance of those who let their hearts outrun their heads. So the first step in the regeneration of the lukewarm is to recognise that the absence of enthusiasm in a Christian is a defect and not simply a defect but a sin, and a sin gravely to be repented of. "So," says the writer, "be in warm earnest and repent." The second fact to be faced is this, that enthusiasm for God is not a self-created but derivative experience. It emerges from a right relationship to the living Christ. And this which was written of Laodicea, and still may be said of many of us, is certainly not a right relationship. "Behold I stand at the door and knock." The King of our faith should be in residence in our hearts, and not in exile. When Jesus moves from the outside circumference of our hearts to the centre, then He brings His own fire with Him. The secret of the burning heart is to receive Christ's holy heavenly love into our souls. He is our divine Prometheus who fetches fire from Heaven to set our souls ablaze. He is the fiery particle of life which kindles within a spiritual conflagration. Even John, the greatest of the prophets, could only baptise with water, it was One mightier than he who possessed the secret of baptising with the Holy Ghost and with fire.

Oh, then, wish more for Him, burn more with desire,
   Covet more the dear sight of His marvellous face,
Pray louder, pray longer for the sweet gift of fire
   To come down on thy heart with its whirlwind of grace.

2. WE REFUSE HIS DEMAND
(*For Lent*)

He went away sorrowful, for he had great possessions (Matt. xix. 22).

This incident is so rich in spiritual suggestiveness that our problem is to know which facet of its truth should be selected for separate treatment. Should one speak of Christ's insight into character, and the courage of His refusal to lower His claims? Or should one dwell on this man's conception of religion as a mere matter of fulfilling legal righteousness? Or, again, are we to stress Christ's view of riches as a hindrance to the good life? These truths are all there and many more besides. Every sentence is a spiritual revelation. Every word carries its own suggestion. We shall, however, pass over all these points in order to concentrate on the essential message of the incident which is the story of a man who, when confronted with Christ's demand, refused to meet it. It is a very sad story and the pathos of it for us consists in this: that it is true to life as we know it to-day.

The tragedy of this young man's refusal is heightened by the nobility of his character, as portrayed by the three Evangelists. He was young, attractive, influential, and popular. His enormous wealth (Luke tells us that he was "very rich") and social prestige gave him ready entrance to the best society. Nor did he waste his money foolishly. He possessed a blameless moral record. He had kept all the commandments from his youth up. He had moral courage of an unusually high order, for it was no little thing he did, when in the public eye he laid aside his social prerogatives to acknowledge the authority of this socially despised Nazarene. He had besides an exquisite sense of humility, reverence and appreciation of spiritual excellence in others. He came to Jesus, "running" and "kneeling" and said "Rabbi." He represents that better type of youth, of refined nature, sensitive conscience, and delicate moral susceptibilities, who has an infinite capacity for the best in life. It is interesting to notice that the three accounts we have of him are placed immediately after Christ's encounter with the children. Is this deliberate, as if to indicate that he belonged to the same order, a man with an unspoiled child-like heart? It is at any rate clear that when Jesus looked upon him, He loved him (one emendation puts it, "He kissed him"), and this He did not because of the possibilities of his character, but on account of his amiable and attractive qualities. That is the type of character the Gospels portray. And there is something more. We have the picture of a man with a disquieted soul. His riches and personal attainments and social perquisites had failed to satisfy the hungry void within. Something was haunting his soul which disturbed his dream of content. He was conscious of a vague want, an undefined defect, of something essential to fullness of life that he was missing. Was it the vision of Christ's richness of nature that touched his slumbering soul, His shining peace and power? *He* certainly seemed to possess the passport to a secret to which he himself was greatly strange. He noticed also that that small circle that gathered round Him had the same mysterious, infectious quality of life. Could Jesus pass over to him that gift which He Himself had described as "eternal life?" How could he get it? What must he do to acquire it? "What lack I yet?"

Let me pause here for a moment to bring this incident up to date. Its interest for us is that it is a description of a type of modern youth in all our churches with which we are familiar. Such people as we have in mind are not rich, nor young rulers perhaps, but these things are only incidental to the story. In every other respect they run true to type. They have been brought up in Christian homes, and have the savour of Christian discipline in their hearts. They have kept their record clean, and have no foul stains on their conscience. They are sensitive in their feelings, courteous in manner, kindly disposed in their affections, and reverent in their attitude to life. They make good sons and daughters, helpful in the home, useful in the world; and are generally favourites. Moreover, they are appreciative of the higher values of life, and respond to goodness when they see it in others. They are full of natural charm and grace which secure for them a safe place in all our hearts. Instinctively their amiable qualities evoke our affection. I am consciously and deliberately colouring the picture, because such types do exist in larger numbers than we suspect. Yet there is some vital defect in their character. It may need an expert like Jesus to lay His finger on their weakness. We feel vaguely that the defect exists, and they themselves are aware of it.

In their deeper moments they ask themselves, "What lack I yet?" Usually they are only dimly conscious of it, yet the misgiving persists. A certain moment comes, a crisis of temptation perhaps, and they feel their lack of strength. Some challenge out of life meets them, and they are powerless to meet it. A vision dawns, summoning them to a life of austerity and high enterprise, and they are incapable of responding to it. When they compare their life with the life of Jesus, its strenousness and vigour and capacity for sacrifice, they are smitten by the sheer stark contrast. Their lives by comparison seem to them to be "tame in earth's paddock as her prize." "What lack I yet?" Let us examine Christ's diagnosis of this defect. What more is necessary to inherit eternal life?

Christ's *first* condition is *renunciation*. Jesus said to him "Sell all thou hast and give to the poor." Let us be careful at this point not to misunderstand the teaching of Christ. These words have often been taken literally and made to mean that Jesus is insisting on voluntary poverty as a necessary condition of eternal life. Strauss rebukes Jesus at this point on the ground that He fails to do justice to the instinct of accumulation. But it is quite a mistaken idea that Jesus is here making riches an insuperable barrier to the Kingdom of God. He is really dealing with a more radical and fundamental issue, namely the problem of all self-erected barriers between the soul and God. The rich young ruler's hindrance happened to be his accumulated riches. Jesus did not err in putting His finger on this spot, and if the truth be told it is still many people's main obstacle to eternal life. Money can be and often is a peculiarly seductive and potent rival to God. It is a kind of alternative Providence. Gold has always wrestled with God. Jesus sets God and mammon face to face as conflicting masters, and Paul roundly lumps covetousness with "idolatry." So the love of riches is a formidable obstacle against which Christ ceaselessly warns us, and when He told this wealthy aristocrat to divest himself of his riches, it was not the cause of the poor He was pleading but the salvation of this man's soul. He was urging him to cut himself adrift from that force that was binding him to earth, and to set his soul free to rise to the upper levels of life. It seems quite certain, judging by the sequel, that our Lord had correctly diagnosed this man's weakness. Yet it is curious and unusual to find one so young mastered by the love of riches, as we generally associate the vice of covetousness with advancing years. Young people are rarely embarrassed with a superfluity of this commodity, and to do them justice they seldom show any great regard for money. But there are other hindrances which with equal effect exclude them from eternal life. One is the ruling desire to run their lives in their own way, without advice or aid from God or man, for the young can be very self-assured. At other times just the opposite is the case. There are those who suffer from natural timidity, a failure in nerve, a lack of courage to face the responsibilities of a higher calling, or to meet the criticism of the social set in which they move. Or again the cause may just be indolence, a lazy complacency, a certain love of pleasure and ease, a mild amiability, a lack of robustness and vigour in the constitution of the will. It is not my province to lay bare the thing that is lacking. That is your business. "Sell all that thou hast." In other words part with the ballast that is gravitating your souls. Strip yourselves bare to the bone. Cut adrift from your besetting weakness. In spirit at least be detached from possessions, illicit desires, and affections; from good works, from even your virtues and attractive qualities. Renounce everything but yourself, and then give that self to God. Only so will you have treasure in Heaven.

The other necessary condition in winning eternal life is consecration to God through Christ. To the injunction to "sell all that thou hast" Jesus adds the exhortation "Follow me." And these two-fold demands convey the assurance to the questing soul that there is a way to the possession of eternal life, but it is a hard way, involving both renunciation and devotion. In inviting us to follow Him He leads us by no harder way than He Himself has trod before us. For did He not strip Himself bare for us men and our salvation? Did He not lay aside His glory, His heavenly privileges and prerogatives, and come amongst us in utter poverty that He might reveal the essential nature of religion, which is a naked relationship between two persons, ourselves and God? And in that act of complete renunciation and devotion He opened all the channels to the inflow of the tides of God's infinite life into His soul, thence to flow forth through Him to refresh and enrich the world's parched and pinched soul. He possessed the secret of eternal life, that life of which Percy Ainsworth thus sings:

> It dwells not in innumerable years
> It is the breath of God in timeless things
> The strong divine persistence that inheres
> In love's red pulses and in faith's white wings.

Eternal life is both Christ's gift to us and His vocation for us. It is that which can only be received at Christ's own hands and which can only be completed in us by devotion to His Person.

It is at this point that Christ challenges the better type of youth in our churches to-day. One has the feeling that with all their attractive and lovable qualities they are too complacent and superficial, too easily satisfied with less than the best. They have not faced the fundamental needs of their own soul nor responded to the challenge of the world's need. They have not heard, or at least not heeded, Christ's call to follow Him where He leads, nor drunk deep draughts of the red wine of His sacrificial life. And it is just this failure to lay aside every weight in obedience to the call of Christ, and commit themselves whole-heartedly, unreservedly, and one-directionally to the supreme enterprise of the Kingdom of God: it is this disregard of the one thing needful that cheats them of the gift of eternal life.

I wish that this story had ended more happily. There is a tradition that it did. Some have even identified Saul of Tarsus with this rich young ruler. It is an interesting speculation, but the Evangelical records give no warrant for resting in this optimistic conclusion.

On the contrary what they tell us is that when Christ stated His demand, this young man refused it. The price was too high and he couldn't face it. Christ puts before him the alternatives of life or death with a frankness which refused to conceal the truth even from so desirable a disciple. We can see them together, this questing candidate for eternal life and the Searcher of the soul's secrets, each playing for the highest stakes. We can see the disciples, Judas amongst them, watching in tense silence this stupendous drama of the soul being played out before their eyes, "amazed" as Mark comments. Then gradually we see the clouds gathering on the young man's face, his bright eager look fading out, as he reckons up the cost. Then with slow leaden footsteps he walks sorrowfully away; "for he had great possessions." We see Christ watch him go, then, turning to His disciples with a look they never forgot, He uttered words which mankind has never forgotten. And it is our own fancy that in the distance we hear the solemn tolling of funeral bells:

> Sometimes I think, and thinking
> Makes the heart grow sore
> Just a few steps more
> And there might have dawned for me
> The blue and infinite sea.

Here is how that prince of preachers, Dr. A. B. Davidson, sums up the whole tragic situation. "A man of high and lovely character, yet feeling that his character was not enough, whose very elevation of character put out its hands, and groped for something better than itself—a man dissatisfied, dissatisfied with the world, and yet unable to give it up; dissatisfied with himself, and yearning for something higher; feeling something in him that was empty, and that yearned and craved to be filled—such a man on the threshold of the kingdom of God, entreated with a look that said He loved him, and yet turning away." Will ye also go away? Let our response rather be, "Lord

to whom can we go but unto Thee? Thou hast the words
of eternal life."

3. WE HIDE FROM HIM

Go, call thy husband (John iv. 16).
And Adam and Eve hid themselves from the presence of the Lord God
amongst the trees of the Garden (Gen. iv. 8).

The art of camouflage, which was so skilfully practised
through two major world wars, is really as old as the
Garden of Eden. It is recorded of our first parents that
they hid from the Lord God in the trees of the Garden.
Their descendants in varying forms have ever since
practised the same type of subterfuge. For a New Testament illustration consider the case of the Samaritan
woman whom our Lord interviewed by Jacob's well. It is
quite possible to interpret this fascinating incident as a
study in the psychology of evasion. This woman's presence
at the well of Jacob, in the blistering heat of the noontide
sun, carrying a heavy waterpot, was an ill-concealed
device to avoid the contemptuous glances and the
embarrassing insinuations of her uncharitable sisters.
The manner in which she conducted her conversation with
Jesus might be regarded as an adroit attempt to parry His
delicate but skilful thrusts. It is just a little difficult to
accept the general view of the commentators that this
pathetic creature was merely a frivolous and coarse-
grained woman, with no insight into the drift of Christ's
conversation, frankly puzzled at the double entendre
underlying His lovely symbolism of running water. The
pains which our Lord took to instruct her, His astonishing
revelation to her alone of His messiahship, and above all
His lofty teaching about the nature of true religious worship, all these things seem to point the other way and
reveal our Lord's respect for her spiritual possibilities.
Whatever this woman's first thoughts were, she quickly
sensed the deep drift of His discourse. The gravity of
His demeanour, the earnestness of His spirit, the rich

suggestiveness of His words, His reference to inner fountains of refreshment "gushing up into everlasting life," all contributed to her growing conviction, that the mind of Jesus was moving on the loftiest levels of thought, that He was dealing with religious realities, and bringing the force of them to bear on her life. With her lively and alert mind she sensed the truth, that this grave Stranger before her was really angling for her soul, and seeking to tear asunder the domino in which her soul was masquerading. She was equally determined to resist those necessary if disconcerting methods of self-revelation and self-exposure. Her pertness and repartee and sarcasm were not so much frivolity as defence mechanism. When Jesus at last brought her face to face with her sordid past and sinful present, she brazenly sought to side-track the moral issue by raising irrelevantly the denominational problem. It was only when she discovered that every form of evasion was futile that she finally capitulated, and in doing so found release and salvation.

Whether or no this is a sound interpretation of this particular incident, at any rate the truth that man's instinctive reaction to the divine initiative is one of evasion abides. Man is a secretive animal. He seeks to avoid the light. He shields himself from the shafts of truth. He hides from himself, holds his fellows at arm's length, and runs away from God. Adam and Eve set the example at the first, and multitudes ever since have followed in their wake. The Bible is rich in illustrations of those who seek God, but it is equally plentiful in instances of those who hide from Him. Consider such cases as these—Jacob fleeing to the bare uplands of Bethel, Jonah hiding from God in the inhospitable wastes of the ocean, Jeremiah sighing for a lodge in some vast wilderness, the children of Christ's generation of whom He complained, "Ye will not come to Me that ye might have life," the Samaritan woman using every weapon in her armoury to deflect from her soul the shafts of divine truth. It is an old story, but it is constantly being repeated. The living Christ still holds converse with our souls, tells us as plainly as He told the Samaritan woman "all things that ever I said or did," and our reaction like hers is to hide from the Divine.

First of all let us consider *why* it is we behave in this way. One obvious reason is the sense of guilt within, which in itself has an estranging influence. We feel that our heart is not right before God, and therefore we take steps to avoid His accusing presence. In similar circumstances this is how we behave towards one another. Even a dog with only an embryonic conscience, when it does wrong, will slink into a corner, and avoid its master's presence. People who wrong each other dislike meeting each other.

Dr. John R. Mott gives an instance from his own experience of a student of his acquaintance who had wronged a girl in a certain village. Every morning he travelled to the city, and although his direct and short route lay through that village he made a detour of some thirty miles so as to avoid any of the associations which reminded him of his guilt. It is our sense of guilt that accounts for our reluctance to come to terms with the divine. Jesus spake a true word when He said, "Everyone that doeth evil hateth the light, neither cometh into the light, lest his deeds be reproved." We also tend to avoid all the associations which aggravate our uneasiness of conscience, and enliven our sense of wrong-doing. Is this not one of the main reasons why we abandon the salutary discipline of public worship? The reasons we give for non-attendance at Church ordinances are seldom our real reasons. It is our worldliness of mind, low ideals and sinful habits which empty the Church pews. "Men love darkness rather than light because their deeds are evil."

Again we hide from God, because we shrink from the ordeal of self-revelation. We try to conceal from ourselves the truth about ourselves. A well-known physician once said to me that he could rarely get a patient to tell the truth. The consulting rooms of eminent psychiatrists are filled with patients suffering from divided personalities whose disorders would speedily disappear if those who suffer from them had the courage to bring their repressed complexes to the surface of consciousness. A large part of the specialists' office is to induce their patients to bring to the light their secret ailment. This process of "exteriorising their rottenness" (as the psychologists put it), is often so difficult that it assumes the dimensions of a major surgical operation. Even people whose condition is not abnormal are reluctant to expose their naked souls to the blinding light of truth. Socrates, the great Athenian, offered ailing humanity one uniform prescription, "Know thyself." Nearly all his skilful dialectic had this one end in view. None of those who were cross-examined by him particularly relished his mental surgery. He was a highly influential citizen of ancient Athens, but distinctly unpopular. Alcibiades confessed that he was at the same time fascinated and repelled by this formidable personality. In his presence he felt that, in intriguing for place and power, he was wronging his own soul, and he confessed that he would have been glad to hear that he was no longer alive. "I was afraid," confessed Adam, *because I was naked*, and hid myself." A great many people in Palestine must have had that feeling about Jesus. The Samaritan woman said to Him, "Sir, give me this water, that I thirst not." When Jesus gave her her first draught of living water what He pressed to her lips was a most distasteful medicine. "Go, call thy husband." One wonders how she liked it. Did the Pharisees appreciate Christ's blistering exposure of their spiritual bankruptcy? Do any of us like to be told the truth about ourselves? We much prefer to seek refuge in subterfuge and concealment.

To expose our souls nakedly to the influence of the divine makes demands we instinctively shrink from meeting. If Christ is to come into our hearts there are certain things already there which will require to be cast out. We shall quite clearly need to be different men and women from what we are now. Many of the things to which we have held on in the past, and which we have grown to like—sinful indulgences, secret compromises, bad habits, fixed prejudices—must be sacrificed. This is so painful and distasteful a process that every instinct of our nature rises up to resent and resist it. All the devils within us will rise up protesting, "Leave us alone, what have we to do with Thee, Thou holy One of God." And as we are creatures of habit, intolerant of change, the acute misery and discomfort which such an inner change involves stimulates our desire to evade this demanding religious issue.

Having considered some of the reasons why men hide from the divine, let us now go on to reflect on *some of the forms which this evasion takes*? When our first parent's eyes were opened, and they knew themselves to be naked, "they sewed fig-leaves together, and made themselves aprons." Since that day man has never ceased to erect screens to protect himself from the nakedness of self-knowledge. He does more than hide from God, he advances justifying reasons to make his evasion plausible. The psychologists call this species of camouflage "rationalisation," the technique by which we make the worse appear the better cause. We seek to be reconciled to our inferior selves by throwing the burden of guilt on to other shoulders. Thus when our first parents fell, Adam did not blame himself but Eve, while Eve in turn blamed the serpent. In modern life this shifting of the blame to others takes an infinite variety of forms, some of which only can be mentioned here. One of the commonest and easiest evasions is to blame professing Christians for our ill condition. Men humbug themselves into the notion that they would readily follow the Christian way of life, if only "those of the way" blazed a clearer and more convincing trail. It is, they allege, the low levels of Christian faith and practice they see around them which account for their lukewarmness. They seek to compound for their personal failure by adopting a policy of detraction. They try to elevate themselves in their own esteem by debasing others. They exalt their pagan coinage by depreciating the spiritual currency with which they are familiar. Whatever truth there be in this charge, it is quite irrelevant to the main issue. Jesus Christ Himself still stands as the gold standard of human worth, and we cannot evade His challenge by hiding behind the alleged inconsistencies of Christians.

Another of these evasions is a refusal to face the exacting

demands of the gospel on the ground of its theoretical difficulties. Men emphasise the perplexities the gospel raises in their minds as a reason for renouncing its claims on their allegiance. The Samaritan woman is not the first "to jump the moral category" by leaping into the dug-out of an ecclesiastical alibi. It is a much less disagreeable and embarrassing procedure to discuss the question of where one should say one's prayers than it is to face the sore point of sexual infidelity. If we can only pretend to ourselves that the gospel is something that can never be understood, then we can reasonably claim absolution from its obligations. No one pretends that the "glorious gospel of the blessed God" is all plain and easy to grasp. It raises its own crop of difficulties. "The well is deep" as this woman justly observed. But it still remains true, that its gifts and boons are easily accessible. The living water is given to us by Christ's own hand, and the thirsty soul has only to stoop down and drink and live. Anyone who uses its intellectual difficulties as an excuse for renouncing its spiritual privileges is merely evading the cutting edge of its demands.

Perhaps the commonest form of camouflage is to exclude the living Christ from our lives by cluttering them with a variety of other interests and concerns. We do not so much deny or reject Christ as crowd Him out. Our hearts are filled with infinite aches and longings, but we do not turn to Christ for heart-satisfaction. We turn to the world and the things the world can give us. We seek the ways of pleasure, gain, the lusts of the flesh and the pride of life, business, social success, politics, recreation, sport. We hide from Him behind these things. Our experience is like that of Francis Thompson,

> I fled Him down the nights and down the days;
>   I fled Him down the arches of the years;
> I fled Him down the labyrinthine ways
>   Of my own mind, and in the mist of tears
> I hid from Him, and under running laughter,
>
>   .   .   .   .   .
>
> From those strong feet that followed, followed after.

And like him, as well as this woman of Samaria, we discover that there is no release for us till we capitulate to the living Christ, who gives to us the only draught that can quench the insatiable thirst of the soul.

In conclusion consider the *futility of this policy of hiding from the divine*. It is futile for the simple reason that the divine is everywhere. We can hide from ourselves, from one another, but not from God. We can hide from one who is here or there but not from One who is here and there at the same time, in short everywhere. Whither shall we go from His Spirit, or flee from His Presence? If we ascend into heaven, climb to the stars, then He who made the stars is there also, and their vast silences are filled with the sound of His voice. If, like Jonah, we take the wings of the morning and dwell in the uttermost parts of the sea, it is only to discover that "He plants His footsteps in the sea and rides upon the storm." If, like Jacob, we flee to the desert, then in our dreams we shall see a ladder stretched up from earth to Heaven, and angels of God ascending and descending upon it. When Jesus rose from the dead He ceased to be a local deity, and became an universal presence, here, there, everywhere, absolutely unavoidable. "The doors being shut, Jesus stood in the midst." How is it possible to hide from such an ubiquitous presence? It is quite futile, because He invades every dug-out of man's devising, penetrates every disguise, tears down every screen.

And what makes this policy of evasion still more futile is the knowledge, that the divine is not only everywhere, but is everywhere seeking us. He is the good Shepherd seeking the one straying sheep, the Father yearning over the prodigal, the Saviour who comes to seek and save the lost. How frequently is this conjunction of events reproduced in our experience? "Then cometh Jesus . . . to the well." "Then cometh a woman to draw water." Jesus is always there before us to offer us another kind of water, of which, if a man drink, he will never thirst again. Dempster in his remarkable book, *Finding Men for Christ*, gives some dramatic instances of the resourcefulness of the living Christ in His search for the souls of the lost in London. The point that impresses the casual reader is the amazing record of the forces that co-operated to achieve the divine purpose. It is astonishing to read of the network of coincidence, the long arm of Providence, the conjunction of casual happenings by which the lost were found by the divine Searcher. How can souls evade the relentless pursuit of the "Hound of Heaven"?

Adam and Eve hid from the Lord, but they did not escape Him. "They heard the voice of the Lord walking in the Garden in the cool of the evening." There is always such a trysting time for God and the soul. In the evening, when the long shadows fall, when the bright light of day is dimmed, the voices of earth hushed, when memory stirs, and gentle thoughts invade our being; in the cool of the evening, when hot passions have spent their fires, and a great stillness falls, and we grow God-conscious and sin-conscious, such moments come to us all. We may try to hide from God, but the wind—the spirit blowing where He listeth—fans our souls, breathes His life into our slumbering being, wakens lost and forgotten desires, makes His presence articulate, speaks to our hearts and says, "Adam, where art thou?" Where do you stand in relation to your soul's salvation? Have you drifted away from the source of all life? Are you seeking the light of His face, or are you erecting screens, fleeing to dug-outs, hiding from the face of God? Mrs. Sarah Gertrude Millin, the biographer of General Smuts, on one occasion visited him to get material for her book. Smuts pulled out his dispatches, opened his desk drawers, which were all filled with papers. "Use them all," he said. "Are you sure there is nothing private there, nothing secret, which I am not permitted to use?" "No," he said. "Go into any room, cupboard, chest, drawer, and do what you like with what you find. Everything is open to you. *There are no secrets here.*"

Have we the courage thus to expose our lives to Christ? Can we say to Him, "Go into any room in my life you please. There are no secrets here." Or do we have secrets?

Are there skeletons in our cupboards? Are there things there we are afraid to tell even to our closest friends, dark secrets which lie like poisonous snakes coiled in the deep recesses of our being? Then let us tell them to Jesus. There is nothing there He does not already know. Drag them into the light of His presence to whom "all thoughts lie open, all desires known and from whom no secrets are hid." That is the secret of release, peace and power. "If we walk in the light, as He is in the light, we have fellowship one with another, and the blood of Jesus Christ His Son cleanseth us from all sin." On bended knees let us offer this prayer to the great Searcher of hearts. "Search me, O God, and know my heart. Try me and know my thoughts, and see if there be any wicked way in me, and lead me in the way everlasting."

4. We Crowd Him Out
(*For Christmas*)

There was no room for them in the inn (Luke ii. 7).

Tennyson once wrote, "We must needs love the highest, when we see it." That familiar dictum looks strange when it is cast into the framework of Christ's earthly career. By universal consent He was and is "the highest, holiest manhood," yet the only crown the world could place on His brow was a crown of thorns. It seems equally incredible when considered in the light of the Nativity. To be sure, there are many strands in that story, some of them of exquisite loveliness. The splendour of that hour did not go unheralded. The star-lit night was filled with heavenly angels and celestial music. Far-travelled Magi and home-spun shepherds offered their gifts and adoration at His cradle. That epoch-making event had its high lights, but it also had its sombre shadows. The cruel leering face of Herod is there lurking in the background, and the indifferent multitudes, who passed unheeding on their way. And here confronting us at the very beginning of the

sacred story is the scurvy treatment meted out to Mary
and Joseph by this nameless yet most notorious hotel-
proprietor in Christendom. It would be a mistake to
regard him as an unfeeling monster. He is not a pathological case. His interest and profit for us is that he
represents an average type of man, to whom the call of
God came, not through angelic visitation such as the
shepherds experienced, nor through the shining of a star
such as guided the Magi, but along the normal ways in
which it comes to most of us, through the routine of
ordinary business. The manner in which that demand was
crowded out by the pressure of other interests, may furnish
a salutary lesson to us on the folly of similar reactions on
our own part.

The *first* suggestion we offer is that the innkeeper acted
in this churlish fashion because of a *desire for gain*. He was
a keen business man with an eye to the main chance, and
these peasant travellers were not the class of customer he
wanted. The Census was a gift from the gods to men like
himself. The highways were crowded with travellers on
their way to honour Caesar's decree. Customers were
many, prices high, and business brisk. He would be a fool
if he gave way to weak sentiment, and failed to catch the
rising market. After all, business was business. If these
pathetic people could not foot his bill, there were plenty
of others who could and would. His immediate concern
was to line his pockets while he had the chance. Let others
do the same if they could.

How modern and familiar is the sound of this plea in
our ears! This hard spirit of commercialism, which lets
the claims of mercy plead in vain and rides roughshod
over the necessities of the needy is one of the major
obstacles in the way of welcoming the Christ-spirit. Our
Lord lists it as one of the rank weeds which choke the
growth of the good seed of the Kingdom. In Luke viii-xiv
He classes money, along with the "anxieties" and "gaieties
of time", as the most prolific sources of suffocation. And
indeed it might seriously be claimed that these other two
largely spring from the same poisonous root. This is not

the only passage in our Lord's teaching which points in the same direction. We are apt to overlook His numerous and solemn warnings against the snare of wealth. His strictures on avarice might almost be said to be one of the main strains of His teaching. His dread of covetousness springs from two main causes. He recognised, as few did, that the love of gold can easily displace the love of God in the heart. Devotion to it becomes a counter-allegiance, an ersatz-religion, a substitute for the support and security which God alone can give. It plays the rôle of Providence in many men's lives, so that the service of God and Mammon are exclusive opposites. The other effect which Christ regarded as equally serious was its power to de-humanise the heart. Tennyson speaks about "the narrowing lust of gold"; and the heart which gives it hospitality makes itself insensitive to the tenderer appeals and more gracious ministries of life. In his grim picture of Mammon where Watts draws with piercing insight a repulsive, brutal, monster unfeelingly and unheedingly trampling under his feet the innocent victims of his greed, the artist has depicted the very soul of this vice. Are we right in thinking that this ancient inn-keeper stands before us as the prototype of that acquisitive spirit which in the interest of mercenary profit shuts up its bowels of compassion against all the claims of human decency, and represents the antithesis of the Christmas spirit? Whether true of him or not, it is certainly true of us, that we constantly need to keep before us the warning of sacred Writ "Let not your heart be hardened by the deceitfulness of riches."

A *second* motive was his *false sense of social values*. These benighted travellers who sought admittance came to him in lowly guise. They were honest and respectable working folk but there was nothing in their appearance to suggest that royal blood ran in their veins. They looked to this man like country, not county folk with royal antecedents. They had slender purses to buy their right of entrance, and no social credentials to command it. It was not a paying proposition to admit those undesirables, when more attractive clients were available. Had some other than these social obscurities sought admission, the case might have been altogether different. Had some of Caesar's entourage, or a representative of the Jewish Sanhedrin, or a plutocrat from the "jeunesse dorée" of Jerusalem sought accommodation, the expansiveness of his house would have been astonishing. How welcoming his smiles; how obsequious his demeanour; how freely his house would have been put at their disposal! But because they looked like home-spun peasants, lacking in means and social credentials, he was hard as nails to their appeal.

Whether this description of the inn-keeper's motive be fair to him or not, it is certainly true to-day, that this un-Christmas spirit of snobbishness crowds Christ out of many a heart. Even in the case of many who formally profess the Christian faith, Christ is exiled because of the tyranny of false social distinctions. The profession of religion is no defence against this pagan spirit. Our Lord spent much of His time in unmasking and denouncing it in the religious circles of His day. Some of His most violent philippics were directed against those who preened themselves on their social status, their ecclesiastical prestige, and their moral correctness. "Ye are they who justify yourselves before men—that which is highly esteemed amongst men is abomination in the sight of God." The Epistle of James discloses the degree to which this taint had spread even in the primitive Christian community, and it is a vice against which we must all ceaselessly be on our guard. To be purse-proud may be more vulgar, but to be class-proud probably does more mischief to the Christian cause. To be puffed up because of our superior advantages in the matter of refinement, breeding, education, culture or social status is quite un-Christian. More than anything else it breaks up the unity of Christian fellowship, discredits our witness, and denies a cardinal tenet of the Christian faith that in the eyes of God all men are equal.

Further, this snobbish spirit in the pagan heart is one of the most formidable obstacles which stand in the way of their acceptance of the Christian message. Snobbishness is not so much a Christian, as a pagan vice. The natural man is a born snob. The social unpopularity of Christianity to-day is in itself sufficient to account for many men's refusal to consider its claims. Those who love fashion more than truth will follow the general drift. If the Christian faith were the vogue, if the people who counted socially were its admirers and supporters, then the worshippers of fashion would be tumbling over each other in their eagerness to give it their allegiance. But the tide is running against the faith for the moment. Only the convinced attend Church ordinances. If others go, it is with an apology on their lips. Christianity to-day is a minority movement, almost a contemptible minority. The big social successes amongst writers, dramatists, film-producers, on the whole do not support it. Those who sit in the seats of the mighty despise it as dope. And all the snobs in the crowd take their cue from them. Jesus Christ still comes, as He came at Christmas, in lowly guise. His feet are amongst the poorest and the lowliest and the lost. He comes in the guise of a beggar, in the cry of a child, in the plight of refugees, in the need of the distressed. He offers us not thrones and kingdoms, but obscure and useful service, not the glittering prizes of life but the incorruptible riches of Heaven, but if it is the fickle goddess of fashion we would fain serve, then naturally Christ is exiled from our hearts.

But perhaps we are doing the inn-keeper a grave injustice. It may very well have been that what accounted for his inhospitality was neither avarice nor snobbishness, but merely pre-occupation. He was a very busy and embarrassed man. He had many affairs on his hands. He had his hostelry to run, the needs of his guests to meet, their meals and comforts to consider. He had to attend also to the clamorous demands of new clients, and make himself pleasant to those already there. He must find time to air the current news and views. There were the affairs of the royal court to discuss, the on-goings of Herod and his butterfly courtiers, the movements of the Roman legions, the latest decrees from Rome, and all the gossip and rumours wafted thither from the great world outside. All the while he was being badgered by fresh requests for more accommodation. Can we greatly blame him, if the pleading voices of two obscure peasants, hailing from a remote and unsavoury town, failed to evoke any response in his crowded life?

How closely parallel this situation runs to our own experience! Is it not the case that, generally speaking, our failure to give hospitality to Christ is due to the fact that our time and interest are already pre-engaged? Our heart's capacity is limited, and if we attend to this we cannot attend to that. Lord Acton once said that "mastery is acquired by resolved limitation." Spiritual mastery is acquired by concentration on things that matter. If we lay our gift on every wayside altar we have neither time nor strength for the service of the holiest. Much of the prevalent irreligion of our time has its roots in the dispersion of our powers. Few men deliberately and of set purpose reject the Person of Christ or repudiate His claims. They are, like this ancient inn-keeper, so completely absorbed in other things that they have neither time nor strength to consider the claims of Christ.

Not infrequently those interests which displace Christ are innocent enough in themselves but quite trivial and ephemeral. The average man's spare time is cluttered up with unessentials—a round of golf, listening to the wireless, television, a game of bowls, a novel, a spot of gardening and so on. We are as busy as bees, chasing these ephemeral bubbles, forgetting the wise saying of the Greeks, "Zeus frowns on the over-busy." Recently I paid a pastoral visit to a woman of wealth and fashion. She had been conspicuous by her absence from public worship. When challenged for this neglect she was engagingly frank. She had a yacht on the river, and her friends came there on Sunday. She had their needs to attend to, social calls to make, endless letters to write, and this was her only day for reading. She was not an unbeliever, she was careful to explain. She believed in the Church. She was quite willing to give a subscription. But to attend the public ordinances of grace, well, it was quite impossible. She was far too busy a woman for that. "Yes," I said reflectively to her: "You have a lot of things to do, but you will notice that all these things are your own things, not God's." But sometimes it is not our own trivial things but the good and even the better that is the enemy of the best. Jenny Lind, the celebrated actress and singer of Victorian days startled the world by withdrawing from the opera stage at the height of her fame, when still almost in her youth. A friend asked her why she did it. "Because," she replied, taking up her Bible, "because it left me so little time for this, and (pointing to the sunset), "none at all for that." Doubtless Jenny Lind by her art charmed, intoxicated, and even inspired, vast multitudes; and also found a fertile field for satisfying her self-expression. But there were other things in life even more important than operatic fame: the things connoted by the Bible and the sunset glory, eternal truth and beauty, and if, like her we want the best we must be prepared to thin out the good and even the better. The Queen Pearl can only be purchased by the sacrifice even of "goodly pearls." "Mastery is acquired by resolved limitation." We must at all costs avoid a repetition of the inn-keeper's tragic blunder. We must not allow the best to be crowded out by the better, the good, or the trivial or the bad. If we do, then these grim, ironic words of the fourth evangelist will be repeated in our experience, "Jesus passed out un-noticed, there being a crowd in the place."

These then are some of the warning lessons which lie deeply bedded in the story of the Nativity. The holy wondrous Babe was born in Bethelehem, and "there was no room for Him in the inn." The Incarnate glory still comes to us, pleading for an entrance into our hearts. Let us see to it, that neither by avarice, pompous snobbishness, nor pre-occupation, do we turn that divine visitation aside. Let us make sure that no hindering influence shall make us guilty of dishonouring the Festival of the Nativity by shut-ting out the Lord of the Feast from the inn of our hearts.

5. WE LOSE HIM
(*For a re-dedication service*)

They supposed He was in the caravan and travelled on for a day, searching for Him among their kinsfolk and acquaintances. Then, as they failed to find Him, they came back to Jerusalem in search of Him (Luke ii. 44, 45, Moffatt).

The incident in which the parents lost the boy, Jesus, in Jerusalem is too well known to be repeated. The mistake was easily made. The pilgrims marching north divided into two separate groups of men and women, and each parent imagined that their Son was in the other company. It was only when they halted for the night that they discovered their loss. It took them roughly three days of anxious search to find their lost boy, and only those who have suffered in like fashion can understand fully their distress. Excuses in plenty can be found for their negligence, but we have no intention of offering them, as we are concerned here with a weightier matter, namely the general experience of knowing Jesus, and then losing Him. Many modern Marys and Josephs have travelled forward on life's journey on the assumption that Jesus was in their company, and then discover later on, to their dismay, that they have lost Him. It is to this class particularly that these words are addressed.

We ought to notice, to begin with, *how easy it is to lose Jesus*. On the first blush such a suggestion might seem to us unbelievable. The initial experience of vital contact with Jesus is so vivid, and the change He works in our hearts so transforming, that we feel that the bond between us is one that never could be broken. Experience, however, has another witness to bear. Somehow our interest in Him wanes, our ardour cools, and the tie between us wears thin and threadbare. This is constantly happening in Church life. Flaming lights become smoking wicks; enthusiastic devotees of the faith become tepid conventionalists; stout-hearted professors become laggard backsliders. We discover to our sorrow that every believing community has its Laodiceans, and even its apostates.

Mary and Joseph went a day's journey, and then they discovered that they had lost Jesus. Many a loving disciple has started out in the caravan of life, assuming too lightly, that Jesus was in his company, only to discover that somewhere on the journey he has lost Him.

Nor should this experience greatly surprise, nor disconcert us. All personal relations are matters of exquisite delicacy, and should never be taken for granted. Unless we are careful to keep our friendships in repair, we lose them. Jealousies spring up which we do not try to allay. Misunderstandings arise we are too proud to correct. Carelessness, indifference, divergence of interest, distance, absorption in other concerns complete the severance. Parents can be so busy here and there that they lose their children. Members of the same family go their own ways, and meet long years afterwards as strangers. In ways like these we lose Jesus. We suppose Him to be in our company when He is not there at all. We fail to take the necessary measures to keep in touch. The drifts of life come between us and Him. We form other ties, and then forget. The delicately poised adjustment of a personal relationship is not made. We grow careless in the things of the spirit, negligent in the culture of the religious life, and gradually lose the divine presence.

Note next how frequently it happens *that the most unlikely people lose Jesus*. No one could have suspected that Mary, mother of our Lord, could have lost her boy. The fact that He was only a boy visiting a great city for the first time surely should have intensified her vigilance. The closeness of the tie that bound them together made it unthinkable that she should have let Him out of her sight for a moment. How much these two meant to each other? This thoughtful boy with His "long long thoughts," and this mother with her exquisite spiritual sensibilities, how near and dear they were to each other. We can well imagine how often in the highlands of Galilee they had held sweet converse, as they talked to each other of the things that lay so near to both their hearts. That such a mother and such a Son should have lost each other seems unthinkable, yet that is precisely what happened.

It is not the sinners only who lose Jesus. Read the Psalms of Israel, or the biography of the saints, and you will be struck by this truth, that frequently the cloud falls which hides the shining of the divine Face. Their recurring plaint is their lapses from grace, their dryness of soul, their dimness of vision, the veiling of the light. It was not a sinner but a saint who wrote,

> Where is the blessedness I knew
> When first I saw the Lord?
> Where is the soul-refreshing view
> Of Jesus and His Word?

It doesn't take much to lose Jesus. The moisture of the breath cast on the surface of a polished mirror will as effectively blot out the reflected image as a black cloth flung across it. A slight deflection from the right path, an unconfessed sin, a peevish burst of temper, the nursing of resentment, an unfriendly spirit, an act of self-will, and blinding mist falls on the soul, and the lovely image of the divine fades from view. Jesus offers to all His friendship, but it is on His terms, not ours. And however close be the tie between us, if we fail to keep step with Him all the way, we lose the sense of His presence. "Let him who standeth take heed lest he fall."

Further, not only do the most unlikely people lose Him, but *they do so in the most unlikely places*. Where did Mary and Joseph lose Jesus? It is rather startling to discover, that they lost Him among holy people, in the holy city, in the holiest spot in that holy city. To lose Jesus amongst His enemies, or in haunts of profligacy is intelligible enough, for what concord hath light with darkness? But to lose Him amongst His own friends, amongst those engaged in religious exercises, and in places devoted to the worship of God, is surely a state of things no one could have anticipated.

Yet this also runs true to experience. I remember on one occasion visiting the Holy Land. I visited the holy city, the holy sepulchre, and the holiest place in the Holy Land, the Garden of Gethsemane. It was an interesting but not a spiritually elevating experience. As I observed the way these holy places were exploited for gainful ends I came away saying to myself, "They have taken away my Lord and I know not where they have laid Him." Holy places and holy people are in themselves no defence against the invasion of worldliness. It is possible to lose Jesus in the externals of religion. A man may recite the creed as Dr. Jowett of Baliol is credited with doing "I used to believe in God the Father." We may lose Jesus listening to sermons. A coalmaster once said to a ministerial friend of mine, "When you're preaching sermons, I'm sinking pits." We may lose Jesus taking the Sacrament, if there be hate and resentment in our heart, as was the case with Judas, when the first Feast was celebrated. A man may do Christian work, take part in Church councils or even sit on a bishop's throne or the moderator's chair, and lose Jesus. To keep in touch with Jesus everything depends on the personal tie. All other things are only means of grace. And if they become ends and not means, they do more harm than good. "There are few," says Frances Havergal, "who go all the way to the Presence. Many are alive enough as to general on-goings, art and music, but so few seem to hear the music of His name." Familiarity with the form of religion, but without knowledge of its force, is one of the certain ways of losing the sense of the divine presence.

Something should now be said about *the tragedy of losing Jesus*. To lose Jesus is the ultimate loss, the final disaster, the supreme tragedy of life, for it means parting with what is indispensable to life itself. There are some things in life whose loss might be regrettable but not calamitous, other things we might part with to our advantage. One of the discoveries we made during the war was the number of things that were unnecessary to a full life. Many of our goods could be listed as mere baggage, impedimenta as the Romans significantly called them. Probably if we all travelled lighter, we should reach farther more quickly and happily. But there are some things we cannot afford to dispense with, and the absence of them is a fundamental deprivation—such things for instance as faith, hope and love. And of all the precious things to which we must hold at all costs and in all circumstances, the most precious is the presence of Jesus. When they lost their Son, Mary and Joseph were deeply conscious of the greatness of their loss. The infinite sense of relief that came to them when they discovered Him in the Temple, and the use of the phrase, "Thy father and I have sought thee in great anguish" (the word is used in Greek of the pain of child-birth), reveal the terrible strain they underwent. A personal illustration may help us here. I well remember once losing my younger son through a nurse's momentary carelessness. He was only three years of age, and he was swallowed up for seven hours in the traffic of a great city in the darkness of a wet winter night. These hours of agonising search, with the heart torn between hopes and fears, were an experience which illumined for me the three day's anguish which tortured the hearts of Mary and Joseph. Do we have any sense of this acute pain in our souls when we discover that we have lost Jesus? If we realised that it is His presence that lights up life and give it all its value, that would certainly be our reaction. We should, like his parents, seek for the lost Jesus in great anguish, because we would feel that to lose Him was equivalent to losing the only light we have in life's dark way, the only Friend that remains with us to the end and beyond the end: in Emily Dickinson's fine phrase, "It is to lose that one fair Face that makes all existence home."

And now finally, if we have lost Jesus, what can *we do to re-discover Him*? One thing we must not do, and that is to repeat Mary's blunder of blaming her Son for the tragedy of separation. "Son why hast thou dealt thus with us?" If we lose Jesus, it is never His fault but ours. He does not move away from us, it is we who move away from Him. The parents of Jesus searched for Him, in the first instance, amongst their friends and acquaintances. There are knowledgeable friends of Jesus, so "far ben" in the secrets of their Lord, that they may put us in the way of re-discovering our lost Lord. But these choice souls are hard to find, and for most of us, human enquiry leads to results as disappointing as were those of the parents of Jesus. There is a surer road to spiritual discovery which is also hinted at in this incident. It is to retrace our steps back to the spot where we first lost Jesus. It may be a humiliating experience, a sorrowful way, a lonely road, but it never fails of success. We must pick up our obedience where we have dropped it. That will probably lead us straight to the Temple. Perhaps we have been neglecting the means of grace. We are all tempted to give up church attendance when we do wrong, or when our spiritual life sags. Yet that is Christ's trysting place, where He holds traffic with the souls of men, and where He is always to be found. "Did you not know that I had to be in my Father's house?" Retracing our steps also means honest scrutiny of our hearts, and a resolute resolve to part with every illicit thing that disaccords with the mind of Christ,

> The dearest idol I have known,
> Whate'er that idol be,
> Help me to tear it from Thy throne
> And worship only Thee.

In the cathedral of Copenhagen there is a statue of Christ chiselled by Thorwaldsen the Danish sculptor. As you approach it the face is hidden. Disappointed at first the guide tells you to approach it on your knees and as you do so the face of Christ looks down on you in great benignancy. We can only rediscover our lost Saviour, when we retrace our steps, confess our sins, practise the disciplines of the spirit, and put ourselves wholly in Christ's hands.

6. We Send Him Away

Then the whole multitude of the country of the Gadarenes round about besought Him to depart from them (Luke viii. 37).

It is a mistake to suppose that Jesus, even in the flood-tide of His popularity, was welcomed everywhere with open arms. It is true that the common people heard Him gladly, that multitudes thronged His steps, that His ministry of teaching and healing stimulated the masses to such excitement that on one occasion at least they would have made Him a king. We are constantly coming across phrases like these in the Gospels, "great multitudes were coming and going, so that He had not leisure so much as to eat." "There were gathered together an innumerable multitude of people, insomuch that they trod one upon another." "He could not be hid." "The whole world," said the priests, "is gone after Him." That was true, but only partly so. There was another side to the picture. Beneath the loud plaudits of the multitudes may be heard the low ominous mutterings of the gathering storm. The members of His own family had already cast doubts on His sanity. His own fellow-citizens at Nazareth had gnashed their teeth, and exerted themselves to assassinate Him. The authorities in Jerusalem had never been friendly, and with the passage of time became increasingly hostile. Even the enthusiasm of the acclaiming multitudes became tepid, and the time was not far distant when they walked no more with Him. Here at Gadara or Gerasa, a Greek province on the other side of the Lake, we have the extraordinary spectacle of a whole community earnestly and unanimously beseeching Him to leave their coasts, as if he were a plague spot or a portent of ill fame. "The whole multitude of the Gadarenes round about besought Him to depart from them." This is so extra-ordinary a reaction to the presence and ministry of the great Healer that it calls for closer scrutiny and diagnosis. Why did the Gadarenes dismiss Jesus in this peremptory and unambiguous fashion? If we can answer that question, we may come closer to an understanding of the reasons why we also send Him away.

To begin with, the *Gadarenes' rejection of Christ was cravenly actuated.* Jesus had done nothing to merit such treatment at their hands, and much on the contrary to make this chilling inhospitality inexcusable. Jesus was no stranger to the Gadarenes. Although this was His first visit to their neighbourhood, His mightiest works were wrought on the other side of the Lake, and His reputation had preceded Him. Many of them must have known Him by sight, some of them perhaps personally, and all of them knew the kind of person He was. They all knew Him to be the prophet of God, mighty in word and deed, who went about doing good. And if any doubt as to His credentials still lingered in their minds, then they had before them an ocular demonstration of His gracious and merciful ministry. He had wrought a notable work of healing in their midst. One of their own citizens had been dramatically and sensationally restored to health. It was not an ordinary miracle. The man in question was a dangerous lunatic who for long had held the whole community up to ransom. Matthew gives us the revealing touch, that where he was "no man might pass that way." He had prodigious strength, bursting the chains with which he was manacled; and escaping to the mountains or dwelling in the rock-hewn tombs, he made the night hideous with his animal cries. He was more like a wild tiger, escaped from its cage, than a human being. Moreover, he was a particularly revolting type. For he tore off his clothes, cut himself with sharp stones, till his naked body was a mass of bleeding and festering wounds. He was indeed a public pest, the terror of children, a horror to women, and the dread of the whole community. That was the situation in Gadara, till that memorable morning when the demon-haunted man came face to face with the Lord of demons, and that masterful word was spoken which quieted the turbulence of that tempestuous nature, and restored the sweet music of reason to his jangled and disordered mind. The Gadarenes were the recipients of that amazing work of mercy. There could be no doubt about the completeness of the cure. They saw the wild man tamed sitting at the feet of Jesus, the naked man clothed, the madman as sane as any of themselves. Were they glad when they saw one of their own citizens so savingly changed? Did they congratulate him on his merciful deliverance? Did they appoint a deputation to

wait on Jesus, and thank Him for ridding their neighbourhood of a serious public menace? Did they pay
Jesus the compliment of producing other malignant cases
that were surely there, that He might extend the scope of
His healing ministry? They did none of these things. They
reacted in an extraordinary and unpredictable way. They
besought Him to leave their coasts.

Why do we send Jesus away? Have we any better
excuse than the Gadarenes? Can we produce a single
creditable reason for this strange behaviour? Jesus is not
an enemy that we should fear Him or resent His presence,
nor even a stranger that we should doubt His credentials.
We know well enough the kind of person He is, what His
intentions towards us are, what He proposes to do for us
and in us, if we allow Him. The rumour of His gracious
deeds of love and mercy has been wafted to our ears. His
influence is around and within us, like the wholesome air
we breathe. His ideas colour all our thinking. His ideas
run in the market place. The impress of His spirit is on
our institutions, literature and art. His Gospel is preached
from every pulpit in the land. And we have felt the breath
of His life in our own souls. Jerome in *The Passing of the
Third Floor Back* has a lovely touch. The jaded pleasure-
haunted woman is met by one who impersonates the Holy
Spirit. With an effort at recollection she said to him,
"Then, we have met before?" "Yes," was the reply,
"there is no living person who has not met with me
before."

Jesus is not a stranger to us and, even if we have no
personal dealings with Him in ways of grace, we are well
aware of the life-changing effects He has produced in the
lives of others. There is not a single community anywhere
throughout the land, where the healed man is not to be
found, and where he does not stand forth as a living
witness to Christ's redemptive power. Knowing all these
things then, why do we send Him away? One reason is
just our fear of the unfamiliar, our dread of the unmanage-
able, our sense of awe in the presence of the supernatural.
There are numerous instances of this feeling of disquiet in

this and the previous incidents. The disciples, confronted with the stupendous miracle of the stilling of the storm on the Lake, "marvelled in awe, saying one to another, 'Whatever can He be?'" An hour afterwards, when He reached the shore, the demoniac "catching sight of Jesus shrieked, and prayed Him with a loud cry, 'Jesus, Son of God most High, what have you to do with me? I beseech Thee, torment me not!'" And when the Gadarenes saw the healed man, we read, "That frightened them." "And they asked Him to leave them, they were so seized with terror" (Moffatt). The sense of being in the presence of powers beyond our control is a profoundly disturbing and terrifying experience, but if we add to that the knowledge that these powers are actively engaged in dislodging us from our sinful fastnesses, that arouses genuine alarm in our breasts. Is our rejection of Christ not due partially at least to what Kierkegaard calls "dread before the good?" E. MacMillan tells about a boy who, when asked to say "A" refused, knowing well that, if he said "A," he would then have to say "B," and so on to the end of the alphabet. So he stoutly registered his declaration of independence, before the remoter implications emerged.

One reason why we send Jesus away is that we are fearful of the ultimate consequences to ourselves of generously welcoming Him. If He is savingly successful in one incurable case, what is to prevent His further conquests? The only safe course is to have nothing more to do with Him. This dismissal of Jesus is our safeguard against any further invasion of His influence into our lives. It is our weapon of defence against the saving overtures of this formidable life-changing Personality. No one, however, can contend that this is a reasonable excuse for dismissing Him.

In the second place the *Gadarenes' rejection of Christ was basely motivated*. We have not yet exhausted the significance of the phrase, "That frightened them." They were afraid, as we have already seen, of Christ's transforming power, of the radical way He could make clean and wholesome disordered and degraded human personality. But they were afraid of something else as well, which struck even more piercingly to their selfish pagan hearts. They were afraid of the charge He would levy on them for continuing His works of mercy and love. Already they thought that they had paid more than enough. In Matthew viii. 33 we read these words: "And they which kept the swine fled, and went their ways into the city, and told *everything*, and what was befallen to the possessed of devils." The "everything" they told was that their pigs were lost, and the incidental and unimportant addendum was that the maniac was healed. The really alarming feature of the situation for them was that the man had been healed at the expense of the loss of their property. And lest a worse thing befell them, they begged Him to leave them. This is not the only instance in the Gospels of this treatment of Christ. Towards the end of His life a much more tragic situation developed. When He scoured the Temple of its racketeers and smashed the system of graft which lined the pockets of the High Priests, we read that "they took counsel together how they might destroy him." Vested interests in vice have always roused the devils of opposition to the gospel, as Paul found to his cost both at Philippi and Ephesus.

This particular incident recorded here has features peculiar to itself. It is one of the best attested historically of all the gospel stories, and belongs to the "Triple Tradition." Yet it contains bizarre details difficult to explain. It has been the happy hunting ground of rationalists, the butt of sceptics, and a problem for the Christian apologist. On the other hand, it should be said that the most modern psychiatrists find in it a rich field of exploration for the new science of the treatment of mental disease by suggestion. Leaving aside, however, its incidental trappings as irrelevant to our main purpose, its central lesson is plain and weighty enough to engage out serious attention. What emerges is the quite modern emphasis which a whole community put on the primary value of property, and the comparatively slender importance they attached to human life. This should strike a chord in us, because we live in a country whose laws are constructed in the interest of property rather than of human life. A man who indulges in petty pilfering to-day is usually punished by law more severely than for maltreating a child, or one who forges a cheque than for wife-beating. In the old bad days a man could be hanged or exported for snaring a rabbit, which did not belong to him. Such things show, not only how far away Gadara, but also the modern attitude is, from the mind of Christ. We speak about the sacred rights of property, but to Jesus nothing was sacred except human life. He was as careless of the rights of property as Karl Marx himself. He allowed the roofs of houses to be ripped open, if this were the only way by which a sick man could be brought to Him for healing. He whipped the cattle out of the Temple and overturned the tables of the money-changers that God's house might cease to be a den of thieves, and become a place of worship for all nations. He drove a coach and four through sacrosanct institutions like the Sabbath, that He might relieve human suffering. Jesus was not an iconoclast nor a revolutionary, holding doctrinaire views of property but, if it came to a showdown between the good of the soul and the goods a man possessed, He never hesitated on His line of action. He was prepared nonchalantly to destroy a whole herd of swine if, in His judgment, their destruction was necessary to emancipate a soul in bondage. And if men send Him away because they prefer their property to their spiritual health, then we can only say that their rejection is prompted by the most unworthy motives.

It ought, however, to be noted carefully that the things which Christ had no compunction about destroying were the things which in themselves were hurtful to man's true spiritual interests, the things which militated against the development of a sane, wholesome, and integrated personality. It is the hoggish instincts, the swinish impulses in us He destroys. It is the vested interests in vice that He liquidates. It should be remembered that swine were regarded by Jews as unclean animals. Josephus is our authority for saying that the owners of these swine in this

Greek region were all Jews. So these Jews were guilty of a double offence, the offence of owning pigs, and also of trafficking with them for purposes of gain. Thus they had put themselves outside the pale as effectively as tax-gatherers. Another fact to be born in mind is that swine were supposed to be the haunt of demons. Putting all these things together, we reach the conclusion that our Lord, in destroying these swine, was in reality invading and destroying the dominion of evil.

It is certainly true of us that, when Christ invades our hearts, it is the demonic forces in us He attacks, the unclean spirits in us. It is our evil passions, our lusts and inordinate affections, our impurity, greed and selfishness, He seeks to expel. Nothing clean, wholesome, or beautiful does He disturb. It is only our pigs He seeks to destroy, the foul passions which disrupt the unity of our inner being. Are we prepared to give up our darling sins, that we may be made whole? Or do we cry out to Christ, like this demoniac possessed with devils, "leave us alone"? If we are not prepared to pay Christ's price for spiritual release, and choose to send Him away, let us frankly acknowledge, that our rejection is prompted by the most sordid motives.

Finally their *rejection of Christ was disastrously culminated.* To the Gadarenes the central tragedy of Jesus' visit to their coasts was the destruction of their property. With eager insistency they hustled Him out of their coasts, lest a worse thing happened to them. In point of fact a worse thing did happen to them, the worst thing that could have happened. He took them at their word, sailed away, and went to the other side of the Lake. Jesus is not the sort of person to outstay His welcome. He is easy to be entreated, eager and able to help, if we let Him. He is anxious to cleanse the Augean stables of our hearts, to bring peace and order into our unquiet and demon-haunted hearts, but if we send Him away, He has no choice but to leave us to ourselves, to our fears, our sins, our spiritual lostness and impotence. That is His unfailing practice. Rejected in one Samaritan village He goes to another. Cast out at

Nazareth He leaves His native town, and so far as we know, His way never led back there again. It may very well be, it often is the case, that He comes again and yet again. For He is very patient, rich in mercy, and with a heart most wonderfully kind. It is always with infinite reluctance and sorrow that He leaves any soul to its doom. He came again to Gadara, as we shall presently see, but meantime He goes away, and that was the major tragedy in their experience. For with His going spiritual eclipse and darkness settled down on that benighted pagan neighbourhood. They had their chance, flung it away by their own folly, and in doing so destroyed themselves. John Ruskin confessed that to him the chief tragedy in rejecting Christ was what men lost by doing so. It has disastrous consequences.

> Christ rejected! Who can tell
> The bitter loss, the darkness fell,
> The withered powers, the yawning Hell
> Of blasted hopes, and frustrate ghosts?

"Let us therefore be on our guard, lest, perhaps, while He still leaves us a promise of being admitted to His rest, some one of you should be found to have fallen short of it" (Weymouth).

III

SOME DIVINE REACTIONS

1. He Comes Again
(*For Advent*)

And again He went out from the borders of Tyre, and came through Sidon unto the sea of Galilee, through the midst of the borders of Decapolis (Mark vii. 31).

THE precipitate and unanimous dismissal of Christ by the Gadarenes raises in our minds the important issue whether or no He accepts this rejection as decisive and final. When we send Him away, does He go for good, without any prospect of His return? In other words, what is the divine reaction to human obstinancy? Is R. M. MacCheyne justified in saying that Christ has last knocks as well as first? Sometimes it would seem to be so. The case of the Nazarenes comes to our minds, at this point. Although bound to them by all the sweet ties of home, Jesus accepted their truculent rejection of Him as conclusive. Perhaps He judged that a second visit would do more harm than good, as it might aggravate rather than soften their evil heart of unbelief. His policy towards Gadara seems to have been entirely different. Disowned, cast out by them, He yet comes again. Mark's narrative makes that abundantly plain. In Mark vii. 31-37, we are told that He left Tyre, struck North to Sidon, then took the ancient road that led from Sidon to Damascus, and skirting the base of the Lebanons, He made a long detour which brought Him down on the east side of the Sea of Galilee in the region of Decapolis. The use also of the curious phrase, "They glorified the God of Israel," indicating as it does that the inhabitants were pagans not

Jews, lends confirmation to this view. This is very interesting and significant information. Why did Jesus return
to a pagan population, that only a little while ago had
cast Him out? The only reasonable explanation is that He
had judged it worth His while to come back again. Something had happened there which had radically altered the
whole situation. We must make room in our thinking for
such a possibility. We must be on our guard against
believing that, as things have been, so they must continue
to be. In point of fact things, attitudes, outlooks are
always changing. There are tides in the affairs of men.
Human nature changes, whole communities, the time-
spirit. Susceptibility to spiritual influences varies and may
undergo in no short time a radical transformation: and
when that happens Jesus comes again. It would be
an interesting study to explore this field further, and try
to account for Gadara's changed spiritual climate.

To begin with we must heavily underscore the *inexorable
teachings of life itself*. Our personal attitude to Christ,
whether good or bad, sinister or welcoming, does not
affect the relentless action of life. It moves forward in its
own impetuous way, quite regardless of our choices,
preferences or prejudices. Whether we come to terms with
Jesus or not, we are compelled to do so with life. Everyman has to live, and face what life deals out to him. He has
to bear life's burdens, solve its problems, share its sorrows,
and endure its tests and trials. A man may renounce
Christ, but he may not and cannot renounce the claims of
life. That is an inexorable demand out of which everyman
is powerless to contract.

The Gadarenes got rid of Christ easily enough, but not
of the burdens He had come to share, and the problems
He was anxious to solve. The entail of life's ills still lay
heavily on their hands and hearts. Was there no disquiet
in their minds, as they watched His boat sail away from
their coasts? Had they no lingering regret that they had
parted with the only Friend who could help them in their
need? Was this healed man the only case of disordered
personality in their midst? Were there no other diseased

folk there that this great Healer could also cure? Was this madman's the only wrecked life in Gadara, its only dark and unlit mind? If they had any doubt on this point, life itself would speedily disillusion them. As the days passed, casting their shadows before, and weighted with their burden of pain and suffering—the grey days of monotonous labour, unlit by faith and hope, with their unceasing pressure of responsibility and care, and failing strength to meet them—were there none who sent out a winged prayer across the blue waters of the Lake, that the great Healer might return? And as the rumour floated over to them of the mighty works done by Him in Bethsaida and Chorazin, which equally well might have been done amongst them, did their whole attitude towards Christ not undergo a subtle and powerful change?

Is it not the case that we seldom realise the significance of Christ for our lives, when first He comes to us? And if we send Him away, is it not due to our failure to grasp His life-changing and life-renewing power? It is only experience of failure that teaches us the value of Christ. Life itself is a cunning evangelist, with many pleading voices. Pain, disease, bereavement, calamity, moral and spiritual defeat plead more eloquently than any human lips. Life itself is stronger than the strongest, and drives us to the sheltering arms of "the Stronger than the strong". That is why in our dealings with the spiritually sick and indifferent we ought to exercise tolerance and a long patience. Every Communion roll has its tragic list of lapsed and useless members. Sometimes we are strongly tempted ruthlessly to purge our rolls, and cut off from the living tree of Christian fellowship the dead wood which lowers its vitality and impedes its growth. Yet we have high authority for restraining ourselves from drastic action. In the parable of the "barren fig tree" our Lord pleads with its executioner who grudges it its room, and would destroy it forthwith, "Leave it alone for this year also, that I may dig about it, open up its roots, let in the air and sunshine, and enrich it with manure." We ought also to give life its chance to drive home its own stern lessons. God has other voices than ours by which to convict the heedless. Some startling arousal may at any time come to them out of life, some tragedy in the home, some public shame, some humiliating moral lapse, some bitter misfortune, or perhaps some glad event which warms their hearts, and unexpectedly the seemingly dumb voice of the soul begins to find an utterance, and there is a quickening movement towards the light. Then the despised and rejected Christ comes back again.

And what applies to the individual is equally true of the age in which we live. The psychological climate of modern life is not favourable to the reception of Christ's claims. His Gospel has no controlling influence on its thought and public action. The gospel is barely tolerated, and it is much if it is not wholly discredited. Our world does not look to the Church either for leadership or inspiration. It is pinning its faith to education, scientific techniques, planned social economy or power-politics. Well, let us test the new method of salvation by its fruits.

How is it working out in experience? Is Secularism producing the goods? Are we satisfied with the kind of world it is creating? Is life becoming sweeter, kindlier, juster, more neighbourly and morally more wholesome for all concerned? Does this age, with its chaotic morality, its suppression of human freedom and threat of atomic war, support the optimism of the social meliorists? Life itself is taking up the challenge, and reducing to absurdity man's baseless belief in his capacity to achieve personal and social salvation. Our Lord Christ's time is coming. He is the only One who can afford to wait. And when our age has drunk the last draught from the bitter waters of experience, He will come again, this time not to be cast out but welcomed as Saviour.

Another influential factor in this changed attitude of the Gadarenes towards Christ was *the presence of the healed man in their midst*. That at any rate was an embarrassing fact for which they must account. A sensational miracle had been wrought which they could not gainsay. One of their own citizens who had been a social liability had become a social asset, and the source of the change was Jesus. No one could get past that fact. It remained there to make its own powerful and availing plea. And as if the deed were not evidence enough in itself, the healed man himself resolutely pressed home its full implications. He put a trumpet to his lips and everywhere publicised the virtue of Christ's saving name. "He went his way, and began to publish in Decapolis how great things Jesus had done for him. And all men did marvel." His witness was like Paul's at a later date. "I was a blasphemer, and persecutor and injurious, but I obtained mercy." This was the burden of the Gaderene's message, "I was before a devil-haunted man, persecuting my fellow-citizens, filling the whole region with terror, injurious to myself and others, but Christ sought me in mercy, restored my mangled body to health, and out of the jangled discords of my disordered mind brought forth a grave sweet melody. What He has done for one such as me He can do also for you all." Such dynamic witness was bound to alter their entire attitude to Jesus, persuade them in His favour, bring them round to His side, and induce them to make trial for themselves of His sovereign grace and wonder-working power.

We need such witnesses to-day to neutralise the prevailing indifference to the claims of Jesus. Some time ago a missionary was evangelising in the hinterland of Manchuria. He was drawing a pen-portrait of the Jesus of history. As he proceeded, he noticed smiles of recognition on the faces of his audience. When he had finished, they said to him with one voice, "We know this Jesus. He has lived amongst us," and then they took him to a grave nearby, and showed the place where the remains of Dr. Jackson were laid. They had recognised the lineaments of the Master in His devoted servant. It ought to be said that exceptionally gifted men and women are not essential for effective witness-bearing. "It is required in a steward that he be found faithful." Of course, if we can secure high-powered personalities like Paul as witnesses, it is all to the good. But the average normal type of standard-bearer, if loyal to his witness, can produce amazing evangelical results. After all, this "Vicar of Christ in Decapolis" was not trained in any of the theological schools. He was merely a social castaway, but he had a plain tale to tell, and he told it with conviction and zeal. And it was not without its effect, perhaps all the more striking that he had been the kind of man he was known to be. A frivolous and light woman of Samaria bore a sincere witness to a change of heart through a casual contact with Jesus, and she was the means of bringing the whole population of the village of Sychar to the feet of Jesus. We have all met and known many ungifted people in our churches who have won striking trophies for Christ through the simplicity and sincerity of their quiet and humble witness. Such witness-bearing is still the major factor in extending the frontiers of Christ's kingdom. "So long," says Dean Inge, "as the Church can produce saints, the gates of Hell will not prevail against it." "Let the redeemed of the Lord *say* so," and hold to it in scorn of consequence, and such vocal witness, backed up by a consistent life, will inevitably dispose the world's hard heart of unbelief hospitably towards Christ.

Before we leave this incident a word or two should be added *on the fruits of Christ's second visit to Gadara*. The situation has quite clearly changed there since His first visit. That is why He came again. He has heard the call of need, and His ears are never deaf to its pleading voice. Is He not the Physician whose tender offices are for the sick and not the healthy, the Saviour who has come to seek and save that which is lost? Depised and rejected, He waits till men's lives are broken on the wheel of life, or some urge within calls aloud for His help, and then He comes again. And when deep calls to deep, He sends forth His word and heals them all. And what a festering mass of human wretchedness confronted Him as He moved about in that pagan desolation! Every kind of disease was there in that unhealthy malaria-swept region—opthalmia, arthritis, palsy, dumbness, and "many others," not to speak of the moral and spiritual darkness that lay like a thick pall over the whole land. They brought them all out, and flung them (a strong word in the Greek) down at His feet, as if in eager haste to collect more cases. And so marvellous were the cures He wrought that "they magnified the God of Israel." Mark tells us that they said to one another "He does everything beautifully." Or as Dr. Moffatt translates it, "He succeeds in everything He does."

All this has an exciting personal reference. The interest of this story for us is that this is not an old tale but a contemporary experience. It may very well be that some of you have, like the Gadarenes and for the same reasons, disowned and rejected Christ. Are you feeling happy about it? Are you glad that you have got rid of this disturbing influence in your lives? You have got rid of Jesus, but have you got rid of your sins, frustrations, personal maladjustments, worries and fears? You know that they are still there, lying like a heavy weight on your souls. Perhaps you are getting older now, a little wiser, and quicker to spot your weaknesses and failures, increasingly disenchanted with your own attempts to save yourselves. Are you beginning to feel that life is getting too much for you, and that you are no longer able to face it, unless some one stronger than life can get beneath you and underpin you, to support your failing strength? Then if you turn to Jesus and seek His Presence, even though you have once disowned or repudiated Him, He will come back again (blessed be His name) and heal all your diseases, redeem your lives from destruction and crown you with His loving-kindnesses and tender mercies.

2. HE WARNS
(*For Lent*)

The Stone which the builders rejected, the same is become the head of the corner—And whosoever shall fall on this Stone shall be broken: but on whomsoever it shall fall, it will grind him to powder (Matt. xxi. 42, 44).

The parable of the Rejected Stone is given in all the synoptic gospels as an addendum to that of the Wicked

Husbandmen. The change in metaphor is so violent that some commentators judge it to be the conclusion of another and different parable. Yet its connection in thought with what goes before is logical enough. The two parables taken together stress the significance our Lord attached to His own Person and also forecast the fate that awaits Him at Jerusalem. Both also predict the certainty of judgment on all His detractors, but in the latter parable this process is carried further and made more explicit. That the parable did not fail of its purpose is clear from the concluding words, "They perceived that He spake of them." The foundation stone referred to here is the purpose of God, that one driving force in human history which is indestructible, and especially that purpose as revealed in His Son.

Our Lord first draws attention to that perverse element in human nature which works against the purpose of God. To illustrate this truth Jesus selects a verse from one of the Hallél Psalms (Ps. cxviii. 22), admitted by the Rabbis to be Messianic, and He adroitly applies it to Himself. The entire Psalm was probably written in post-exilic days during the rebuilding of the Temple, and registers anew God's purpose to make Israel the vehicle of His grace and truth to the world. Alas, the proud pagan nations, cutting and carving the world as they saw fit—not knowing the divine Architect's plan—had set at naught God's beneficent design. They rejected the religion God designed to be the key-stone of history. And now Israel herself in turn is perpetrating the same colossal folly and crime. And not for the first time either. In the previous parable Jesus recapitulates the spiritual history of Israel, and charges the whole nation with the maltreatment of every sincere prophet that had made plain that divine purpose. Their crowning infamy was the fate they were reserving for Him whom they knew to be the Son and Heir, in whom that Purpose was fully revealed.

This is one of the puzzling enigmas of human nature. Tennyson writes, "We needs must love the highest when we see it." Nothing could be further from the truth.

Indeed mankind's instinctive selection of the inferior, when presented with an ascending scale of values, is one of his most distinctive and disconcerting traits. This is clearly seen when applied to other spheres than religion such as art, music, literature or education. "Love of the valleys is everywhere," writes some one, "only the few love the heights." Beethoven is sacrificed for jazz; Shakespeare for low comedy, the classics in literature for Wild West stories or detective novels, and the cultural values of education for those of utility. The glittering rewards go to the prize fighter, the cinema star, the popular comedian, while poets starve in garrets, and scientific research-workers subsist on a meagre pittance. If the people love to have it so, is it any wonder that Christ, in whom all the treasures of wisdom, and knowledge are hid, is despised and rejected of man? Can superlative spiritual excellence bid successfully for the suffrage of mankind against such preferred inferior competitors? Indeed Dr. Marcus Dods puts forward this general repudiation of Christ as one of His claims to be what He is, "the lonely greatness of the world." "Rejection by the builders was one of the marks by which the foundation chosen by God was to be identified." How is it possible for many men, living the lives they do, and possessing the tastes and preferences they have, to see any beauty in Christ that they should desire Him? The unpopularity of Christianity must not entirely be laid at the door of the Church. Its failure to make a general appeal is not wholly the fault of its defenders, but largely and in the main due to dislike of the things for which Christ stands. The Jewish race is not the only one guilty of rejecting what God accepts, and repudiating what He honours.

Our Lord next passes on to lay bare the consequences which take place when men reject God's corner Stone. The first effect is maiming or loss. "Whosoever falleth on this Stone shall be severely hurt" (Weymouth). At this particular point Jesus is not discussing the fate of those who deliberately and defiantly reject the Stone through an evil heart of unbelief but rather the case of those who do so through misunderstanding, thoughtlessness or inattention to the gravity of the matter on hand. Such people never dig beneath the surface for foundation on which to build the house of life. They live unexamined lives, and refuse to come to terms with the demanding claims of Christ. None the less the results of this neglect are very grave. They have yet to reckon with the Stone they disregard. It is still there, everywhere there, a massive obstacle blocking their self-chosen path. If they accept it, and build upon it then, as Peter writes in his first Epistle, they are built as lively stones into the living Stone, and become the "new Israel of God." But if they "disallow" it, it trips them up, bruising and wounding them. It becomes a "Stone of stumbling."

What Jesus would have us learn here is the inevitability of His influence. He abides as a permanent factor in our character and destiny, even when we put Him from us. He remains to challenge us, even when we try to ignore Him. He is so much a part of our environment, our literature, our institutions, our social and individual lives, that we cannot shake off His hold upon us, even if we would. And if we try to do it, then something delicate, sensitive and fine dies in us. Something happens to us and in us which leaves life maimed and impoverished. Our faith loses its bloom, our ideals their lustre, our conscience its sensitiveness and our inner life its tone. And what is true of us individually holds good also in the wider relationships of life. Not even the Church is immune from this judgment. If she seeks to build on any other foundation than that laid by God, then she suffers loss in a depreciated spiritual currency, and a diminution of her serviceableness. The Jewish Church is not the only one of which it can be written, "He will let out His vineyard to other husbandmen who shall render Him the fruits in their seasons." And in the life of nations all efforts to construct an international order, which ignores Christ's principles of justice, good-will and universal brotherhood, will meet with frustration and loss. The late Arthur Henderson tried to establish through "the League of Nations" a system of law which would accord with the principles of the Christian faith. He failed, and on his death-bed said: "They wouldn't take my way. But they will have to come back to it—after waste and suffering that cannot be measured." The truth is, that life will only back one way, and that way is Christ's way. Every other way leads to a dead end. If we, from whatever cause, follow any other way, we merely hurt ourselves.

Christ proceeds now to consider the case of those who defiantly flaunt His way of life, and deliberately and insolently work against it. They find themselves in a much more serious position than is the case of those already considered, and their fate is correspondingly much more disastrous. The Stone which hitherto had remained an inert object, blocking the way of advance, and tripping men up, now suddenly becomes alive, full of purpose and the power of initiative. It is, as if it had the power of levitation. It lifts itself up on high, and hurls itself with crushing force at those who scorn it. "On whomsoever this Stone falls it will grind him to powder." Our Lord without doubt had in His mind the metaphor used in Daniel ii. 34, where the sacred writer uses those words: "A stone was cut out without hands which smote the image upon his feet that were of iron and clay, and brake them to pieces." The underlying idea is that the power which moved this massive stone to fall upon and crush to pieces those instruments of idolatry was not cut with human hands, but was God's strange work. It was God's vigorous reaction to human apostasy.

Stripped of all metaphor, what Jesus is doing here is issuing this solemn warning, that the despising of the living Stone and the setting of it at nought is of all forms of human folly the most disastrous. For God Himself has made His Son to be the foundation Stone of all reality, and no human being can with impunity tamper with that ground pattern of existence. Jesus in this passage is for all practical purposes identifying Himself with the *moral order of the world*, that order which is as fixed and as immutable as the natural laws of the universe. To fight against it is virtually to fight against God Himself. It carries with it, when violated, the power to defend itself, and like a boomerang to hit back, and grind to pieces its violators. Its action is immediate, automatic, and inescapable. All far-seeing men in all ages have paid tribute to its majesty and sanctity. It is one of the main themes of all great novelists and dramatists. This law constitutes the high tragic element in Shakespeare's plays, in the writings of Dickens, Victor Hugo, Hardy and Hawthorne. Even simple peasant people, like the primitive cave-dwellers in Malta, paid tribute to its inescapable force. It runs, like a recurring theme, through all the prophetical books of the Old Testament. Amos is vehement in his proclamation of its inexorableness. In one grim passage he describes the fate of those seeking to escape from its grip. "It is as if a man should try to flee from a lion and a bear met him, or went into a house and leaned his hand against a wall and a serpent bit him." The rejected Stone, crushing the body of its violators, is our Lord's picturesque way of describing the same truth. Paul called it, "the wrath of God," by which phrase he means to express the automatic action of divine judgment. In Romans i he furnishes some striking illustrations of the avenging power of outraged spiritual sanctions. The wrath of God is executed on these flagrant violators of His will by deprivation, through the darkening of their minds and their complete insensibility to moral issues. God gave them up to this, that and the other abominable practice, till at last they reached the lowest rung in the ladder of degradation, of "glorying in their shame."

This principle of divine causality runs all through the spiritual order of the world. Anyone can test the truth of its operation in his own experience. Sometimes on the broad field of history it receives dramatic confirmation. From time to time leading personalities have appeared who in a great way have sinned against the light, and one by one their star has been quenched in darkness. At one time Napoleon bestrode the world like a Colossus, but his meteoric career was rudely cut short. Victor Hugo makes this comment on the end of his career. "It was time he was stopped. This single man was counting for more than the whole of mankind. The hour had come for supreme incorruptible justice to take notice. Napoleon had been denounced in the Infinite, and his downfall decreed. He was obstructing God. Waterloo was no mere battle. It was a change of front on the part of the universe." And the historian Fisher in the same vein writes, "He came across a force, imponderable by his scales and measures, and possessing, as it proved, infinite power of recovery and recoil." Hitler set himself forward as the new Messiah, scorning Christ's sacred name, and disallowing all His values, and in an incredibly short time came the recoil, the shattering and conclusive blow. So it has been from the beginning, is now and ever shall be. Firmly laid in the bedrock of time is this foundation Stone, tried and precious.

That truth ought to be proclaimed with vehemence in the councils of nations. The history of the world is just the record of its reactions, favourable or unfavourable, to the Living Stone. The Jewish race is not the only one that has perished through its rejection of the Living Stone. Indeed the history of the world is strewn with the wreckage of nations which lacked the binding power which respect for the moral order of the world could alone produce. Nearly all of them, according to Toynbee, perished through war, and war is just the active judgment of God. How stands it with our Western civilisation to-day? That is a question men are everywhere eagerly canvassing. Does it contain within it survival-value? Or must it mingle its dust with other civilisations that are dead and gone? The answer to that question is bound up with its attitude to the corner Stone which God has set in Zion. One of the most disquieting features of modern civilisation is the extent to which individual nations and groups of nations repudiate the Christian Gospel and ethic, or indeed any absolute standard of moral behaviour. If there be any truth at all in this parable of Christ, then it seems fairly certain that along that line lies ruin and extinction. And

no armaments designed for security purposes, nor scientific
discoveries, nor human skill and political sagacity can
avert the inevitable doom awaiting it. Lacking the
binding force which adherence to an absolute morality, or
better still to the revealed will of God in Christ, can
secure, it will either decay from within or be wrecked
from without by its inherent weakness. Along what
direction then does hope for the future lie? The way of
retrieval is roughly outlined in Psalm ii. There in pic-
torial language the Psalmist exposes the folly of nations
cutting adrift from allegiance to the living God. There
also God announces His inflexible purpose to enthrone
His Son, and give Him world-dominion. Finally He makes
plain the only way to avoid disaster and ruin.

> Now therefore, ye kings, be wise
> Be instructed, ye rulers of the earth.
> Serve ye Jehovah with fear,
> Kiss ye His feet with trembling,
> Lest, indignant, He hurls you to ruin,
> For soon will His anger blaze.
> Happy all who may take refuge in Him.
>
> (J. E. MacFadyen)

Here then is an aspect of Christ's teaching to which we do
less than justice, and to which we ought to pay earnest
heed. Here in this parable He reminds us of His profound
significance for human well-being, as well as warns us of
the serious and solemnising consequences of neglecting or
rejecting His claims. This represents Christ in His most
formidable aspect. It is striking to notice how, as His life
drew rapidly to a close, His teaching grew in austerity,
and His demands became more uncompromising. He is
no longer the "gentle Jesus, meek and mild" but the
Judge of men and nations, "out of whose mouth went
forth a sharp two edged sword." Here in this parable He
presents Himself as the Man of destiny, the touch-stone
of life, the watershed of history. The happiness or misery,
the success or failure of life, hinge on our right or wrong
relation to Himself. He becomes a savour of life unto life,

or of death unto death. That living Stone which is Christ is made the head of the Corner, whether we like it or not. His writ runs through the whole moral universe, "His will is the bed-rock of eternal reality," His Gospel is the judgment-seat of men and nations. If we ignore His claims, we suffer serious loss; if we reject them, we destroy ourselves; if we accept them they are to us the power of God unto salvation. Wherefore also it is contained in the Scriptures, "Behold, I lay in Zion a chief corner stone, elect, precious; and he that believeth on Him shall not be confounded. Unto you therefore which believe He is precious; but to those which be disobedient, the stone which the builders disallowed, the same is made the head of the corner, and a stone of stumbling, and a rock of offence, even to them which stumble at the word, being disobedient."

> What lives by life that is not thine
> I yield it to Thy righteous doom;
> What yet resists Thy power divine
> Oh, let thy fire of love consume.

3. HE SUFFERS
(*For Passion Sunday*)

And being in an agony He prayed more earnestly; and His sweat was as it were great drops of blood falling down to the ground (Luke xxii. 44).

Another of the divine reactions to human sin is vicarious suffering. This is indeed startling and unexpected. So far we have conceived the divine reaction to men's folly and estrangement in terms of patience or chastisement. The view that human sin creates divine suffering is distinctly new and peculiarly Christian. That sin wounds and lacerates the heart of God is a conception which we owe to Christ alone. The measureless nature of that suffering finds its completest expression in the experience our Lord Himself endured in the Garden of Gethsemane. In saying this we are not forgetting His most bitter and desolating

Cross, yet, dreadful though that ordeal must have been, it may be justly contended, that in the experience of the soul of Jesus He anticipated and drank in the Garden a cup even more bitter than that which was offered Him on the Cross. All the Evangelists stress the dreadfulness of the Gethsemane ordeal. Each adds some characteristic touch to deepen the shadow that rested on the soul of Jesus. As He entered the Garden He Himself is represented as saying, "My soul is ringed round and round with sorrow" (the Greek word is very strong), and He adds that His sorrow was such that it brought Him to the verge of death. It was literally "a killing sorrow." Matthew tells that "He began to be sorrowful and sore troubled." The latter is an unusual word and is sometimes translated, "off the ground," "Out of His native element," "far from home," implying the distress created by a perplexing and disturbing situation. Mark adds that He was "amazed" or "stupified." It is Luke who describes His sufferings as an "agony" and the word is here used in its classical sense as a wrestling for the mastery. It is Luke also who tells us, doubtless with a physician's eye for bodily detail, that beads of perspiration glistened on His brow, and fell to the ground like "gouts of blood." No one can read these narratives without gathering the impression that the normal tranquility of our Lord was rudely shattered by an overwhelming emotional storm. The foundation of His being was broken up, and the floods that poured through His soul left Him spent in body and spirit. The description of this experience we have in the Gospels gains in impressiveness by its deliberate restraint and understatement. The starkness of the description heightens our sense of its realism, its solitariness, its personalness, and extreme anguish.

Is it possible for us to enter with any degree of sympathy and understanding into the anguish of that lonely Sufferer? Can we penetrate the thick veils which shroud the mystery of dark Gethsemane? How comes it that He who an hour or two ago in the upper room exhibited a soul bathed in tranquillity should now be swept by a paroxysm of grief and desolation? Why those strong cryings and tears? What means this bitter cup He was asked to drink? Can we name its ingredients? Or must we just stand outside, and look on, and wonder and surmise?

The complete answer to this question can certainly never be uttered by human lips. There is a depth here no human plummet can sound. The sufferings of our Lord beneath the olive trees of the Garden are His alone, and are incommunicable. We could only enter fully into them, if we shared His nature, and that is obviously impossible. Yet there are certain suggestions and stray hints which can be caught and followed and, so long as we remember that we are only groping, feeling our way tentatively, we may find in them something which will bring us into closer sympathy with Christ, and be of help to us in our hour of need.

Let me begin by asking if the near prospect of the physical ordeal of the Cross was an important factor in His sufferings. It is usual to attach little or no importance to this ingredient in His cup. We have, however, no business to make little of this. To undergo this ordeal was no light matter for those concerned. It represented Rome's most superlative refinement of cruelty. Cicero describes it as "crudelissimum, deterrimumque supplicium," "cruelest and foulest of punishments." And in Christ's case there were all the infamous accompaniments of torture, obloquy and reproach. Jesus was familiar with every item in this horrific ordeal. Can we conceive what the cumulative effect of such a prospect would be on One so much in love with life, so highly strung and so sensitive to pain and reproach? We do not wish to exaggerate the importance of this aspect of His ordeal (the Gospels only lightly touch it, and never with a view to engaging our sympathy), but we ought to recognise it as a subsidiary factor in His cup of suffering.

But to come closer to our subject a second suggestion we would offer was the intense realisation by Jesus of *the diabolical malice and treachery of the human heart*. It is not without significance that the overwhelming sorrow that swept the soul of Jesus in the Garden emerged after Judas had taken the sop, and gone out into the night to betray His Lord. Did Jesus in that hour see spread before Him the accumulated acts of perfidy that were to follow? Did He envisage the general defection of all His disciples? Did He anticipate the collapse of the bulwark of Roman justice by mob violence and lynch law? Did He forecast the rejection by the Jewish religious leaders, not only of their own heritage, but of their Messiah. It is not too much to assume that all these sinister forces at work at this moment were present in the mind of Jesus, and added to His bitterness. From time to time He had prophesied to His own disciples the course of events now transpiring. What was new was the intensity with which they were now realised. It was the concentrated fury and violence of the assault that "amazed" Him. He was under no delusions about the nature of man. In Mark vii He had psycho-analysed the human heart, and His analysis of the ingredients He found there were not flattering to man's nature. But it was only now, when that mass of vitriol bespattered Himself, when He was made to drink that Hell broth to the dregs, that the full measure of human depravity came home to Him with a sickening intensity. Rather than drink that cup He started back in horror. "Let this cup pass."

As an extension of this thought Warburton Lewis makes an interesting suggestion which is here given for what it is worth. He suggests that Christ's cup of sorrow was *His conscious precipitation of human sin*. His presence in Jerusalem was bringing human perfidy to a focal point. He who had come to save men from sin was actually by His presence accentuating their sin. The greater His loyalty to the divine will the more diabolical became the reaction of His enemies. Let Him but continue His present line of action, let Him pursue still more closely the curve of God's will, what would follow then? Would all the dogs of Hell be let loose, and the cup of man's infamy be filled to the brim? That, according to Mr. Lewis, was Christ's dilemma in the Garden, and the cause of His uncertainty.

He was fearful, lest His fearless witness would be the occasion and the cause of man's darkest, deadliest crime. He was agitated and distressed, lest His faithfulness would precipitate the foulest crime with which the pages of history could be sullied, the crime of slaying God's beloved Son. Their infamy would be not only suicidal but deicidal. His life, in the ending of it, would be man's final damnation. Anything rather than that. "Father, let this cup pass."

There are, however, other and more convincing reasons for Christ's distress in the Garden. Surely an important element in His agony was the tension set up in His mind between the claims of His natural will and that of His Father. It is a mistake to suppose that the doing of God's will came to Him as a matter of course. On the contrary, spiritual obedience created for Him His chief temptations. The ordeal in Gethsemane was really an intensified form of the temptations in the wilderness. And these royal temptations set up stresses and tensions in His soul which were reflected in His body. In the Garden as in the wilderness a part of the struggle lay in His uncertainty as to what the will of His Father was. Could it be His will that His Son should endure this dreadful ordeal? Was there no other way of accomplishing His redemptive purpose? Could it be that a loving Father whose delight was in His Son, who at all times honoured and exalted Him, should appoint a path for Him, attended by such conditions of humiliation and shame? Was this the Father's cup at all, not only in the sense that He was giving it to His Son to drink, but also in the sense that He Himself was in it too? Were these the problems that agitated the mind of Jesus in the Garden? Was His agony a struggle to see the will of God and, having seen it, to do it in despite of His own will? He certainly appeared to be temporarily in the dark, like some one feeling His way to the light, presented with alternative courses, and not quite certain which to take. He wrestled with His problem all alone, in an agony of distress, He fought His doubts and won His way to certainty, as we all have to do, by effort, reflection, waiting upon God and by a spirit of willing obedience.

But having said all this the conviction persists that we have not said enough. There is more to His agony than the natural recoil from the Cross, or the sin that brought Him to the Cross, or uncertainty about God's will or reluctance to do it. We feel that the conviction of the Church has not erred in attaching an expiatory value to Christ's sufferings. The agony of Jesus sprang not merely from the necessity of contacting human sin, but from bearing it on His heart that He might bear it away. He was elected of God to bear this monstrous load of being made sin for us, of standing in the sinner's stead, of bearing the foulness and shame and guilt of the human heart, of suffering in Himself all the consequences of human sin, even to the "death beyond death" of suffering the eclipse of His Father's face. Is it a wonder that He cried, "Let this cup pass." We can only look on afar off upon a sacred sorrow we can never understand. No human being who is a part of the sin-problem can by any stretch of imagination conceive what it meant for the sinless Son of God to bear our sins on His own body, that He might bear them away. "The waters," writes Chadwick, "into which He sank, were defiled as well as cold. Only thus can we explain the agony and the bloody sweat. And as we, for whom He endured it, think of this, we can only be silent and adore."

Ere we leave this Garden of suffering, let us linger for a few moments longer to gather some practical lessons that will relate our lives more closely to the challenge of Gethsemane. The first lesson we learn here is the *cost to God of the forgiveness of our sins*. It cost His Son tears and gouts of blood and the long drawn out agony and dereliction of the Cross. There is a cheap and facile way of regarding forgiveness, as if it were a legal process, or the cancellation of some outstanding debt, or letting bygones be bygones. "God will forgive sins," said Heine lightly, "that is His métier." We forget that forgiveness is an intensely personal experience, involving the restoration of ruptured fellowship. When such is the case, then reconciliation can never be easy, either for the forgiver or the forgiven. Even in the Old Testament it seemed to those who experienced it a wonderful thing which called forth a lyrical response of wonder, love and praise. In the New Testament it is an awesome and incredible thing, because it carries in its heart a passion such as Jesus felt in the Garden of Gethsemane. Let us never forget that if the assurance of the divine forgiveness is ours now, it is only so, because our Saviour once agonised in the Garden and still suffers in our room and stead.

But this is not the only lesson we learn there. It is not enough that our only response to the passion of Christ should be the acceptance of the gift of forgiveness. "I am washed in the blood of the Lamb," cried an ecstatic convert. "Did it hurt?" asked the preacher. "No," was the reply, "The hurt was His, the joy mine." "If it hurt Him it ought to hurt you," said the preacher. That must be so, if we accept the challenge of Gethsemane. If we love Christ, and our fellowmen in Christ, we, like Christ, must become "the bosom friends of sorrow." We must in out own way, like Him, become sin-bearers. Parents who love a wayward prodigal son cannot wash their hands of him. They must share his burden of lostness, perhaps bear the burden of his debts, certainly of his shame and guilt. And those who love Christ must drink His cup of anguish for the sins of men. Some one once found Henry Drummond, after a night of interviews with students, showing all the symptoms of illness. His face was drawn and tears were in his eyes. To one expressing solicitude he explained: "I feel filthy and sick with these men's sins." To accept this burden is heavy and costly, making big demands on one's spiritual reserves, but it is the challenge of Gethsemane. "Shall that body which has a thorn-crowned Head, with gouts of blood glistening on its brow, have delicate, pain-fearing members?"

But that is not all. Something else remains to be added. When Jesus passed through His fiery ordeal in the Garden, He was not alone nor forgotten of His Father. "There appeared an angel from Heaven strengthening Him." Even on the Cross the cry of dereliction was followed by the quiet prayer of trust. "Father, into thy hands I commend my spirit." And one of the great compensations of partaking in "the fellowship of Christ's sufferings" is the accompanying assurance of the Divine presence. Carlyle tells of an experience of his young boyhood's days, when his father had to carry him across a stream in full flood by a narrow plank. He carried him face downwards, so that the little fellow had a full view of the foaming, swirling waters beneath. "If it had been my mother who carried me," he said, "she would have given me her face to look at." When God asks us to share the burden Christ bore, and, in our capacity as sin-bearers, to plunge into the dark stream of human guilt, we shall not be companionless. God Himself will be with us and carry us through. He will give us His face to look at, and on His face will be a smile.

4. He Entreats
(*For the Lord's Supper*)

Behold I stand at the door and knock; if any man hear my voice, and open the door, I will come in to him, and sup with him, and he with Me (Rev. iii. 20).

This text is a simple but moving exposition of the ministry of divine grace. It is a revelation both of the passion of the eternal Christ to invade and possess the human heart, as well as of the methods He takes to achieve this end. It was spoken first of all to a tepid and torpid Church in Asia Minor, but the incidence of its application is universal. "If *any* man hear." The suggestion of our text is that the reason for this inhospitality is blindness. The Laodiceans were seemingly unaware of the realities of the situation confronting them. If they were alive to the fact that the Lord of the Churches was being kept outside, could they have behaved as they did? "I counsel thee to buy of me eye-salve that thou mayest see." So His first word to them is an arousal, a call to attention, a curt, challenging, stabbing word. "*Behold.*"

Do we, any more than they, grasp the significance of the spiritual situation? Do we realise that the Divine is making pleading overtures to us? Who is this Figure that patiently stands at the door of our hearts? He is not an obscure nonentity, but the Lord of Heaven and earth. He is not a casual Stranger, making a fleeting contact, actuated perchance by motives of curiosity, but the best-known person in time and eternity who is seriously concerned with our highest interests. He is not a mendicant craving an alms, but the opulent Benefactor of the human race who has come here to make poor mortals rich. Do we know that this is how matters stand, and have we grasped its significance for us? He is obviously afraid that we don't, so He calls on us to tear down the screens from our eyes, and see what is there. "Behold." In this saving engagement He is undertaking on our behalf, observe closely His behaviour and attitude.

He stands. He keeps on standing. He does not move away. He stands, "in lowly patience waiting to pass the threshold o'er." But why does He keep on standing? Why does He not crash through the fast closed door? Why does He not storm the bastions of human personality, and plant there the flag of His will? "All power in Heaven and on earth is given unto Him," why then doesn't He use it? Human beings, with infinitely less power, have resorted to this course. The kings and captains of the earth bring violent pressure to bear on those who resist their sovereign will. Dictators give short shrift to those who oppose their mandates. They meet resistance with the prison, torture and concentration camp. Priests have before now invaded the rights of conscience and enforced obedience. Even parents whose children seriously cross their will for them have been known to turn them out of doors, and disinherit them. Only Jesus wholly respects the sanctities of human personality. Only the Divine waits on free human consent. He steadily refuses to play the rôle of a burglar, and coerce the unconsenting will. He is resolved to preserve at all costs the Father-son relationship, that spiritual tie, formed on the basis of free choice, which makes this relationship what it is. So He refuses to exercise physical pressure of any kind beyond what we choose to give. In terms of the spiritual contract which He Himself has made with us, the only course open to Him in the presence of human obstinacy is to *stand* where He is, without.

He knocks. He does not stand passively, doing nothing. He makes His presence felt. He tries to persuade us to a better course. He tries to make us hear, to influence our minds, to move our hearts, to stir up our consciences, to act upon our wills. Many and ingenious are the methods He uses. Sometimes He knocks loudly, again gently. Sometimes He thunders on the door, as when He rouses us by the hammer strokes of calamity, or the rude thrust of death. Sometimes the moral failure of our lives rouses us to a sense of our need of Him, and again some glimpse of everlasting beauty kindles the flame of aspiration in our hearts. The face of a little child, the memory of lost innocence, the call of human need, the reflection of Christ's glory in the face of a friend may be enough to rouse us to responsive action. Perhaps the appeal of His holy and venerable Cross may evoke our wonder, love and praise, as nothing else does. Indeed and in truth the Cross is His loudest knock at the door of the human heart. It is the topmost note in His call, His last and final overture of grace, His most persuasive technique for breaching the walls of human resistance. In active ways like these, along the lines of Providence and grace, He tries to reach us, and neutralise our indifference and opposition.

And then *He waits*.

He waits on our response. Having taken the initiative, and made plain by His behaviour His desire towards us, He meanwhile can do no more. He cannot open that door from without, because there is no key-hole on the outside and no handle. *It must be opened from within*, by the voluntary action of the person within. And he may refuse to do it. The most persuasive and pleading voice of the Holy Spirit may go unheeded, or if heard may be disregarded. Walter de La Mare has a beautiful little poem which he calls "The Listeners," in which he tells of a traveller on horseback who, weary and spent, alighted at a house on a distant lonely moor. He knocked on the closed door gently, then louder and still louder, but he got no response. "Is there anybody there?" he called.

> No one descended to the Traveller,
> No head from the leaf fringed sill
> Leaned over, and looked into his grey eyes
> Where he stood, perplexed and still.
> "Tell them I came and no one answered."

Is that the response we propose to make to this far-travelled heavenly Visitor? Why do we not answer the divine appeal eagerly and promptly?

Is the explanation that of the little boy who hazarded the suggestion, that perhaps "they were too far ben the hoose"? Or is it that there are too many voices there already to pay heed to the still small voice of the Spirit? Or are we too much pre-occupied with our own affairs to attend to divine concerns? Or are we too given over to a life of pleasure to give hospitality to a thorn-crowned King? Whatever the explanation be the result is the same. The King of love is exiled from His throne. Yet here is the mystery and wonder of His grace. He does not go away. He still waits. What a strange blend of long-suffering love, amazing humility, and undiscourageable patience this picture presents! What a strange reversal of the great and lowly, of the Giver and receiver: "If I were God," writes A. E. Whitham, "I would look for a throne, on which to reign. He looks for a Cross on which to die. If I were on top I would think of my rights. He thinks of His burdens. I would count success in my servants, He in His service." But let us reverse the picture and assume that the door is opened. What happens then? This happens.

He enters. "I will come in to him," He enters into our hearts, and takes up His abode there. This is a great mystery, but it is not unfamiliar to us, because it is confirmed on the levels of human experience. What does friendship mean, save that another's life is implicated in ours and ours in his? The mystical experience of I-Thou, and Thou-I is involved in all true relationship with others. The divine experience is just the higher friendship. The experience of grace is just the living Christ taking up His abode in our hearts. Regeneration and santification are just the travail of Christ's Spirit in our hearts. In the parable of the Vine and the branches Jesus elaborates this mystical idea. "I am the Vine, ye are the branches. He that abideth in Me and I in him, the same bringeth forth much fruit." It was a leading idea of Paul. His favourite expression was "In Christ." He also uses the other phrase with equal relevance. "Christ in me." "I live, yet no longer I, but Christ liveth in me." And speaking to the Galatians he wrote, "My little children, of whom I travail in birth again, till Christ be formed in you." When we open the door of our hearts, the Spirit of the living Christ takes possession of us, and floods our inner being with the love, the light, and power of His presence. Upon that willing response of ours there follow the effects of that indwelling.

He enriches and satisfies. "I will come into him and sup with him and he with Me." Life under Christ's control is here represented under the figure of a feast. It was one of Christ's favourite symbols for describing the fruit of entrance into His Kingdom. A feast suggests exhilaration, high spirits and unrestrained joy. When the Lord Christ enters He sets all the joy bells ringing in our hearts. That is worth thinking about. For one's first instinct is not to regard religion as a feast but a fast. It expresses itself in prohibitions, repressions, negations. Most people, especially young people, mistakenly regard the Christian faith as a killjoy that wet-blankets the innocent pleasures they enjoy, and freezes the warm genial currents of the heart. There is no warrant for this bleak outlook in the Gospels. Jesus compared His religion to a feast, and when His disciples took Him at His word, and behaved like people intoxicated with joy, the Pharisees were scandalised at their improper behaviour. Jesus defended their uncoventionality on the ground that they were like guests at a marriage party, and were acting *in propria persona.*

"Can the children of the bridechamber mourn, while the Bridegroom is with them?" Further there is satisfaction as well as enrichment, when we sit down with Christ to the feast of grace. For the Lord Himself gives us all we need from His groaning table. He satisfies our souls as with marrow and fatness. And beyond all these things there are the other elements present at a feast among friends—the good fellowship, the freedom and spontaneity of self-expression, the mutual sharing of each other's interests, reciprocity of feeling, the give and take which flows freely among those whose hearts are in accord. "I will sup with him and he with me."

Finally all this that we have been saying ought to make plainer to us the meaning of the Sacrament of the Lord's Supper. One truth at least leaps out of the heart of it, namely this, that as it is a feast and not a fast we are not mourning over a dead Master, but rejoicing in a living Lord. There is a real Presence presiding at this Feast. This is more than a memorial feast. His word to us is not, "Do this in remembrance of my death, but of Me, continuing and persisting through my death." "Here, O my Lord, I see Thee face to face." So this is an occasion for joy and not for sorrow. This is a Eucharistic feast. "This is the hour of banquet and of song." It ought to be stressed that this is the Lord's Supper, not ours. It is His Table which He has spread with His own hands. We are His guests at this Table, invited here by the Lord of the Feast Himself. This is His trysting place which He Himself has chosen to meet with His own. Therefore it is above all an agapé, or love-feast. Think for a moment of that first sacrament celebrated in the upper room at Jerusalem. It was the supreme experience in the life of those early disciples. It was the one shining hour that was the flower and crown of all their hours with Jesus. It was a love-laden, love-intoxicated hour. It was as if all the grapes of life had been distilled into one foaming cup and pressed to their lips by the hands of Christ. He had come into them and supped with them and they with Him. So it ought to be with us too. For this is the Communion of the Lord's Supper, a communion of hearts, a sharing of lives, a mutual give and take. There is not much, to be sure, that we can give Him, but what we give He gladly takes. We can only give Him our love, our contrition, our sorrow for our failure, our desire to do better, our utter need of Him. All the gifts are really in His hands, and as we take them from Him in trust and love, into our weakness He comes with His strength, into our poverty with His riches, into our sinfulness with His purity and into our emptiness with His fulness. By faith we partake of His body and blood, "to our spiritual nourishment and growth in grace."

As we close, let us stress once again the importance of this conditioning clause, "If any man hear my voice and open the door." All Heaven's blessings are contingent on the quality of our response. That applies to Christians as well as non-Christians. We cannot forget that this exhortation was addressed in the first instance to the members of the Laodicean Church. Christians to-day may likewise lose their first love, may grow lukewarm, fall from grace, grow heedless to the voice of Christ and harden their hearts against Him. Or perhaps, what is commoner, they may give Him only a meagre and partial hospitality. They may open the outer door and admit Him across the threshold, but no further. They may practise a vestibule religion. They may exclude Him from all the other rooms of their house, from the living rooms, where they meet their friends, and play with their children, and discuss business, or eat or sleep. Is this the reason why so many communicants find participation in the Lord's Supper so unsatisfactory an experience? It seems to do little for them in the way of comforting or empowering or enriching their lives, and they wonder why? They would not wonder long, if they turned a quick ear to Christ's call, ceased giving a negative or reluctant obedience, and swung their hearts wide open to His gracious indwelling. Then indeed life would become a joyous festival, a holy communion, a rich and satisfying banquet. "I will sup with him, and he with Me."

Even so come, Lord Jesus.

5. He Saves
(*For Holy Week*)

And Jesus said unto him, Verily, I say unto thee, To-day shalt thou be
with Me in Paradise (Luke xxiii. 43).

Did Jesus, I wonder, ever have any doubt about the
virtue of His death? Did He not sometimes ask Himself,
if the sacrifice on the Cross were not a vain oblation? If
He did (and there is no warrant in the Gospels for any
such supposition), this incident must have set His mind
finally at rest. He had not long to wait for convincing
evidence of the power of His sacrifice. The first fruits of the
Cross were reaped, while He was still suspended on its
cross beams. He demonstrated conclusively in the conversion of the dying malefactor the power of the Cross for
reparation and retrieval. On the Cross He cried, "I
thirst," but when He pressed the cup of salvation to this
outcast's lips, and he drank deep and long, Jesus saw of
the travail of His soul and was abundantly satisfied.

We know nothing about the penitent malefactor save
what Luke records. Tradition has it that he was a Galilean.
We cannot tell whether his offence was political or social,
whether he was an anarchist or a brigand. His crime
must have been very serious to have brought him to the
place where he was. For he was judically examined by a
Roman tribunal, and duly sentenced to crucifixion. Rome
sometimes made mistakes, as in the case of Jesus, but
as a rule their justice did not miscarry. We may take it
for granted that, to quote his own words, "we receive
the due reward of our deeds." The long arm of Roman
law had flung these two together, the holy undefiled Son
of God, and the hardened, lawless Jewish brigand. No
two such contrasted types had ever before been suspended
together on a Cross of shame, nor such startling results
achieved. To the one it was an opportunity of retrieving
a desperate moral situation; to the other, a field for the
exercise of His sovereign mercy and grace. The one sought
the Lord, while He could be found, called upon Him while
He was near; the Other responded by gently drawing him

within the circle of grace, and making him a member of the household of faith. This is such a beautiful and spiritually suggestive incident that we must examine it in greater detail.

First of all we have here *a wonderful penitence*. To realise how remarkable it was, we must remember that this malefactor belonged to the criminal type. Now this is not the kind of soil that is at all favourable for growing or culturing the lovely flower of penitence. Edgar Wallace, in his autobiography, says that in all his experience of the criminal type (and he had a unique and specialised knowledge of this class), he never found a single instance of such a person showing any signs of regret, or sorrow, or shame for his foul past record. He found rather countless instances of stolid indifference, of sullen resentment, of boasting self-exhibitionism, almost of glorying in their shame. We have all read accounts of public executions, where the criminal behaved gaily, acting a part as if he were a public hero, drawing the limelight on himself, and rejoicing in his brief if dubious claim, to singularity. Indeed Wallace goes so far as to suggest that the key to such people's character is vanity. If this be remotely true, it makes this man's penitence all the more remarkable. How differently he behaved from his fellow malefactor, whose reaction to legal justice and punishment was probably more usual. He cursed and taunted, and bared his teeth like a trapped animal. But this other brigand quickly dropped his taunts, became quiet, subdued, thoughtful, and exhibited all the marks of regret and sorrow. Not only so, he also did what must have cost him immense courage to do, he made public confession of his crimes before an unsympathetic and hostile mob. This is indeed a wonderful penitence, and we can only marvel at the power which produced it.

What is there in the Cross that convicts the soul of sin? What did this man see and feel there, that he should suddenly be induced to set his whole life in reverse? Was it a certain distinction in Christ's bearing, the sheer goodness that suffused His countenance, His superiority to all rancour and bitterness, the love that broke through in mighty torrents, His selflessness, His thought for others, His transparent innocence, the dim and growing sense that He was suffering vicariously for others? Was it just the total impact of Christ's spirit on his life, the grandeur and magnanimity of His soul? Who can tell? The Cross has a secret power all its own of reaching the heart. George Eliot in her *Middlemarch* speaks of the effect produced on the soul of one man by the incredible magnanimity of another. This is how she describes it. "A kind of regenerating shudder went through his frame, and made him feel as if he wanted to begin a new life." On kinglier levels that is perennially true of the power of the Cross. Men still look on Him whom the world pierced and mourn for their sins. The Cross has a strange and unique power of subduing the hard heart of man. Some time ago the Student Christian Movement printed a little book called, *A Gentleman in Prison*. It tells the story of a Japanese criminal who was condemned to death. As he was awaiting the day of execution, and having nothing else to do, he picked up in his cell a New Testament which some American ladies had thoughtfully provided. He read its pages idly and listlessly, till he came to the story of the Crucifixion, in which the prayer occurs, "Father, forgive them, for they know not what they do." This stabbed his sleeping conscience broad awake. "It was as if a five inch nail had been driven through my heart." The Cross has wonder-working power. It brought this malefactor to a state of brokenness of heart and to a public confession of his guilt. What the chastisement of law could not do, what the memory of lost innocence was powerless to accomplish, what the terrible effects of sin were impotent to create, Jesus on His Cross, who only prayed and suffered and loved, divinely achieved. "A regenerating shudder went through his frame and made him feel as if he wanted to begin a new life." A wonderful penitence indeed.

We have here also *a wonderful faith.*

"I question," writes Calvin, "if since the world began there has ever been so bright an example of faith." These are striking words, and make a sensational claim, but there is substance behind them. One sometimes wonders what gave rise to this soaring faith in this man's heart. He was not a spiritually minded man. His entire past record seemed to rule out such a possibility. Any spiritual sensibilities that he once possessed must have been calloused by his criminal career. Moreover his first contact with Jesus took place in circumstances which were not calculated to evoke or stimulate trust and faith. The universal despisal of Christ would tend to depress rather than excite any germ of faith that might have been there. All the circumstances of Christ's death were working against faith in Him. Our Lord's own countrymen had cast Him out. The religious leaders had judged Him worthy of death. Pilate had judicially endorsed the judgment of the people. His own disciples had deserted Him. The malefactor's brother in crime had gone over to the enemy, and swelled the ranks of the detractors. It is difficult to believe, when the judgment of the world is against you. And Jesus was all alone on the Cross, despised and rejected of all men. Moreover there was little to encourage faith from the situation in which Jesus was placed. To cherish faith one must have an object to excite and sustain it. And there was little here that did either. This man met Jesus first of all in the hour of His mortal weakness. He met Him hanging, like himself, on a Cross, a bound captive, a helpless victim, a tortured dying prisoner, exhausted and spent, seemingly as powerless to help as he was himself. Yet here is the miracle of this man's faith. He hailed Him as the Friend of man, when all his friends deserted Him. He justified Him, whom His own nation condemned. He acknowledged Him as King of Heaven and earth, when the Roman soldiers jested and sneered at His kingly claims. He saw in the ruin before Him a nameless majesty, in His shame a resplendent glory, in His abject defeat the promise and fulfilment of victory. He saw beyond the Cross to the throne, beyond His rejection to His coming coronation, and he cried out, "Lord, remember me when thou comest into Thy kingdom." Was there not divine irony in the fact, that the only person at the last who really glimpsed the royalty of Christ in the garb of His humiliation was a despised and condemned malefactor. "Truly there are last that shall be first."

Faith in Christ is easier for us than it was for him. We see to-day the circumstances of Christ's death through the light of our Easter faith, and that has completely changed our whole perspective. We now know, as this man could not have known, save through a God-given blinding flash of spiritual intuition, that the Cross was our Lord's hour of glorification. To quote Calvin once again, as he speaks of the victory of the Cross: "There is no tribunal so magnificent, no throne so stately, no show of triumph so distinguished, no chariot so elevated, as is the gibbet on which Christ has subdued death, and the devil, and trodden them under His feet." We know that now, and we know even more than that. We know that our Lord once crucified has gone up on high, and taken His seat at the right hand of God, from which He will come to judge the quick and the dead. Faith is comparatively easy for us compared with this man. Yet one sometimes wonders if we, with all our clearer light and greater knowledge, can produce a faith in our glorious Risen and Exalted Lord which, for its quality and completeness, is comparable to this man's faith in the despised and rejected Nazarene. A wonderful faith.

Finally, we have here *a wonderful salvation.*

This is the jewel which eclipses every other gem that flashes in the Saviour's diadem. To this man, in his dying agony, with all his sins scarlet on his soul, and in response to his prayer, Jesus, all powerful even in death, bent low His ear, heard his prayer, and drew him gently within the circle of His saving love. He took him from a fearful pit and from the miry clay, and set his feet upon the rock of salvation, establishing his way. "To-day," He whispered in his ear, "to-day shalt thou be with Me in Paradise." We need not enquire too curiously what these words mean. At the least they mean the certainty of salvation, full, free, immediate, complete. *"To-day," "In Paradise,"* "*with Me.*" The place was not uncertain. "*In Paradise,*" with "the spirits of the just made perfect," with those who had "come out of great tribulation and washed their robes and made them white in the blood of the Lamb," in the place of peace and blessedness,

> where no storms come,
> Where the green swell in the haven is dumb
> And out of the swing of the sea.

And the hour of his release would not be long delayed. "*To-day.*" Ere the sun set he would be far away to "where beyond these voices there is rest," beyond the leering faces of the priests, the indifference of the soldiery, the execration of the mob, the obscenities of his fellow-conspirator in crime . . . beyond it all in the calm and peace of Paradise. Did ever stormy day set in such tranquil light? And the best was yet to come. He would be *with Jesus.* He would be for ever with the Lord, "With me," never more to be parted. That alone were Paradise enow.

> How know I that blessedness befalls
> Who dwell in Paradise,
> , The outwearied heart refreshing
> Rekindling the worn-out eyes?
> Nay much more than this I know,
> For this is so, Christ is there.

"The reality of redemption," writes Weinel, "is to feel one's self at home, safe and blessed." A wonderful salvation!

Who can estimate the comfort of this story? With such an example before us, no one need despair of salvation. This is a crucial instance. If Jesus can take a sinner like this, who has sunk to such depths of degradation, and wash away his guilt in His own most precious blood, so that his once filthy soul becomes "clean as the air above the clouds or on the middle seas" then we can set no limits to what the same Jesus can do for us. With this example before us, we now know that Jesus "is able to save to the uttermost all that come to God through Him." But if

there is comfort in this story, there is also warning. God's
best gifts can be wrested by the ungodly to their own
undoing. It is possible to use this incident in such a way
as to support the delusion, that a death-bed repentance
will atone for a life-time of wrong-doing. God is certainly
very gracious, and will not turn aside from those who seek
His face in penitence at the last. This is, however, a very
different thing from sinning, that grace may abound. It
is a very dangerous course we take, if we use this story to
support the view, that we can live any kind of rotten life
we please, provided we die with a prayer of penitence on
our lips. Those who cling to this delusive hope should
remember for their warning, that there were two malefactors on two crosses at Calvary, and while the one
blessed God and died in peace, the other cursed God, and
went forth to His Presence, with all his sins scarlet on his
soul. The old divines were fond of explaining the contrast
in these words. "There was one malefactor on the Cross
who repented, that none might despair, and only one,
that none might presume."

6. HE STAYS
(*For the New Year*)

I will never leave thee nor forsake thee (Heb. xiii. 5, 6).

This is an ideal New Year's text. It is brief and easily
remembered, arresting and bracing. It covers all con-
tingencies, occasions and circumstances. It is our Lord's
own promise, countersigned by His authority, and backed
with all His energies and powers. It was the promise
given of old by Jehovah to Joshua, as he faced the hazard-
ous task of conquering the Promised Land (Josh. i. 5).
But the same promise comes to us now with all the added
weight which our Lord by His death and exalted life
gives to it. It is good for us to have the assurance, as we
face the uncertainties and responsibilities of another year,
that besetting us behind and before is the Love divine

that never lets us go. Its singularity can only be fully appreciated when it is set down in the context of human relationships. Here are some of the thoughts which this contrast suggests.

Sometimes people *leave us but do not forsake us*. Is this not one of the most familiar experiences of life? There are those who love us—the companions of our youth, loyal friends, our kith and kin—who never forsake us, but are often compelled to leave our presence. Life itself is a ruthless divider, thrusting its claims between our natural instinct to stay and the necessity to depart. Life, as we know it, is a series of partings, and in every parting is the shadow of death. The world calls to the children in the home, and however close be the tie which unites children to parents the call of the world must be obeyed.

So from the hearth the children flee,
   By that Almighty hand
Austerely led; so one by sea
   Goes forth, and one by land,
Nor aught of all men's sons escape from that command.

Duty calls, and we must yield our reluctant homage to its imperious summons. The son notes his ageing father, his whitening hair, his feebler step, his stooping shoulders, and the urge rises within him to stay by his side to be his comfort and support. But even as he so resolves, the strong hand of the State lays hold upon him forcibly, and calls him to sterner tasks than ways of peace. The daughter would fain stay within the shelter of the ancestral home, but the urge of nature and the call of love send her forth to build a home of her own. Death calls and all of the sons of men must bow to its inevitable decree. So we go, each our separate ways, in obedience to the trumpet call of life or death. We all go, some on longer, some on shorter voyages, others on the journey from which there is no returning. Yet, although we leave those we love, we do not of necessity forsake them. We keep them in our thoughts. We remember them in our prayers. We write letters to them, exchange gifts, pay frequent mutual visits, share richly in each other's interests and doings. Even death is misnamed the great Divide. For we believe in the communion of saints. We believe that its dividing walls of silence are pierced by spiritual presences. Those whom the hand of death claims do not forsake us, nor we them. "At the going down of the sun and in the morning we will remember them."

Some people *both leave us and forsake us.*

The Bible is replete with illustrations of this double treachery. The worthless Absalom, whom his father loved not wisely but too well, leaving his father's side and setting up a rival throne, is a case in point. The Prodigal Son in a mood of rebellious wantonness left his father for a far country, and forsook the ideals of his home for a career of riotous living. Demas, once Paul's friend and co-worker in the Gospel, grew weary of Paul's society and flung aside the faith that had once knit their hearts together. "Demas hath forsaken me, having loved this present world." The lessons that Scripture teaches, experience enforces. One is pained and puzzled at the accumulation of S.O.S. messages transmitted from time to time across the radio. "Will so and so go to such and such a hospital, where a father or mother or near relative is lying dangerously ill? Last heard of in such and such a place three, five, ten fifteen years ago." What has happened to create these dividing walls, so that children have become so indifferent as to cease to care whether their parents and near relatives are dead or alive? At the marriage altar solemn vows are made to take each other in sickness or health, for better or worse, till death do them part. Why then has divorce become epidemic? Why can't husbands and wives live as heirs together of the grace of life? Why those chronic misunderstandings, those tragic alienations, those bitter household divisions, those violent ruptures of the marriage bond? There are reasons and reasons; but whatever the reasons, the tragic issue of these inconstancies is that those who ought to be bound together in the bundle of life have come both to leave and forsake each other.

Again there are those *who forsake us but don't leave us.*

R. L. Stevenson tells of two sisters who lived together in Edinburgh. "The pair inhabited a single room. From the facts it would seem to be double-bedded. And it may have been of some dimensions, but when all is said it was a single room. Here our two sisters fell out—on a point of divinity belike. Never a word, black or white, was spoken between them from that day forward. You would have thought they would have separated. But no, whether from lack of means or the Scottish fear of scandal, they continued to keep house where they were. A chalk line drawn on the floor separated the two domains. It bisected the doorway and fireplace, so that each could do her cooking without violating the sanctity of the other. For years they co-existed in a hateful silence. Their meals, their ablutions, their friendly visitors were exposed to an unfriendly scrutiny. And at night in the dark watches each could hear the breathing of her enemy." That is merely an extravagant illustration of the kind of spirit that too often stains the beauty of human relationships. Hosea could not find it in his heart to part with Gomer, but she had forfeited all claim to be his wife. Judas forsook Jesus in mind and heart long before the final betrayal, but he remained a member of the disciple band to the end. There are husbands and wives who honour the legal tie of marriage, but have long ago grown indifferent, and barely tolerate each other. There are children who are in the home but are not of it. They use their home merely as a convenience, as a lodging in which to sleep, or a restaurant in which to feed. They have forsaken the home, but not left it. People may exist together but not live together. There may be propinquity but no affinity, physical relationship that is devoid of spiritual sympathy, neighbourhood without friendliness. "It is not where I breathe, but where I love, I live."

It is in the light of these limited or false human relations that we are in a position to assess adequately the singularity of the divine promise, "I will never leave thee nor forsake thee." Let us consider first of all the significance of the second clause of this text, "I will never forsake thee." Looked at superficially we may feel disposed to question the soundness of this promise. Sometimes through an imperfect apprehension of God's ways with us it looks to us as if He did forsake us. But that is never really so. Sometimes in His dealings with us as sons He may see fit to discipline us sorely, but it is in love He disciplines, "that we may be partakers of His holiness." Sometimes He withholds from us for a season the light of His countenance, but that is merely to exercise our faith, that we may seek Him more earnestly. The sorrows which darken our lives and bring to us the sense of being forsaken are but "the shade of His hand outstretched caressingly." Even sin, the greatest force in life which separates from God, is not strong enough to effect a permanent rupture. His grace is mightier than all our sin, and the Cross of Christ is our guarantee that God's love will never forsake even the greatest sinner. He never forsakes us.

See how true this is! Sometimes we speak about God coming to us, as if He had temporarily forsaken us. In reality all that that means is that we become aware of a Presence that has never forsaken us. On earth Jesus was a Person spatially limited. He was merely a local Deity. When He was in one place He could not be in another. He left this world that He might inhabit all worlds. He went out of here to there, that He might go into the everywhere. "It is expedient for you that I go away, for if I go not away the Comforter will not come to you." He left our side that He might dwell for ever in our hearts. He went away that He might be always present. He ascended up on high that He might make good the promise, "Lo, I am with you alway, even to the end of the world." Sometimes it is a profitable exercise to consider some of the things God cannot do. He cannot deny Himself. He cannot make a man bound and free at one and the same time. He cannot tell a lie. He cannot square a circle. And here is another thing He cannot do. He can never say "good-bye" to the soul of man. "I will never forsake you."

Let us turn now to the first phrase in this text, "I will

never leave you." This is not simply a repetition of the second phrase for the sake of emphasis. Hitherto we have used it in a merely spatial sense, as if emphasising the truth that He never leaves our side. And we are justified in attaching this meaning to it, because it is abidingly true. Strictly speaking, however, it is not the exegetical meaning of the word "leave." It has a specialised meaning in the original Greek. The revisers translate it imperfectly, "I will never fail thee." Luke uses the same word in Acts xvi. 26, where, speaking of the Philippian earthquake he says of the prisoners, "their chains fell off" or rather, "let go their hold." The word "never" is also used intensively. So we may sensitively translate the whole passage, "I will never never let go your hand." Or rendered colloquially it would then read, "I will in no circumstances whatever let you down." How rich and suggestive our text now becomes! It gives us the comforting and strengthening assurance that the eternal Christ will not only never leave our side but that He will always stand alongside to help us in all our need. He will never let us down.

We need an assurance such as this glorious, divine promise gives for these lives of ours, lit up, it is true, by examples of superb loyalty, but also shadowed by dark and base betrayals. For the truth is, that we are constantly letting ourselves down, by our inconsistencies, insincerities and frequent lapses from grace. We are always letting one another down, friend a friend, parents their children, children their parents, lovers, husbands, wives. Sometimes we do it thoughtlessly, from cowardice, or mercenary motives, or deliberately and of set purpose. A man came to me recently, over sixty years of age, who had worked in a certain firm for forty-eight years. His service and character were above reproach. But a new head had taken charge of the firm and he wanted cheap labour. He turned this man into the ranks of the unemployed with a week's wages and without a word of thanks for all his long and faithful service. In the intimate relations of the heart where men and women give themselves to each other for better or worse, experience furnishes many tragic cases of the betrayal of trust and loyalty. Against that dark background of human inconstancy the divine faithfulness shines like a star of hope. He never lets us down. When Peter found himself engulfed in the turbulent waters of the Galilean sea, he cried out in his sore distress, "Lord, save me" and immediately Christ stretched out his hand and held him. It is a parable of life. When we also sink in life's alarms, and all its waves and billows go over us, at such times as we cry to Him in our great need, we find beneath us the supporting arms of the Eternal. He never lets us down. We may let Him and His cause down, and we often do. We may deny Him as Peter did, betray Him as Judas did, forsake Him as all the disciples did when He needed them most; but He never denies nor betrays nor forsakes us. We may be faithless but He remains faithful. We may be fickle and inconstant but He remains always the same, yesterday, to-day and for ever. This is the experience of all who have put Him to the proof. Paul once found himself a stranger in a strange city. He was summoned to appear before the bar of Caesar on a charge of treason. He was a lonely man in sore need of friends to support him in his trying ordeal. He complains that at that moment all his friends forsook him. All of them except One, of whose faithfulness there is no end. "Notwithstanding the Lord stood with me, and strengthened me." No one was more competent than he to bear this witness: "No one who trusts in Him will ever be disappointed." That was long ago, but listen to this testimony from the last war. It was given by General Dobbie, the Governor of Malta during the Malta blitz. "I cannot attempt to describe what I owe to the Lord Jesus during my Army service and before. The knowledge that it is to Him that I owe my personal salvation has given me a peace that nothing else has been able to disturb, while the companionship and help He has been able to give during all these trying years in Malta has been very real and wonderful." He never lets us down. Have we not the witness of this truth within ourselves? Has any one of us ever trusted in Him, and been put to shame? It was the proud boast of Michael Croz, the great Alpine guide, "This right hand of mine has never let a man down." And with greater truth Jesus said of those whom God had given Him, "Nothing will be able to pluck them out of my hand." When Donald Hankey lay dying, with his last breath he was heard to whisper, "*Teneo et teneor.*" "I hold and I am held." "I will never let you down."

Here then is a message of cheer and hope with which to confront the New Year. We are facing a future that is uncertain and insecure. What it holds for us, of weal or woe, of happiness or sorrow, of austerity or plenty, no one can predict. It may be that we shall be called upon to pass through dark valleys of tribulation, cross stormy seas, scale mountains of difficulty such as is suggested Joshua had to meet in his conquest of Canaan. We may be harassed by fears as we look into the future. Our writer in the context of this text suggests two fear complexes, the fear of economic insecurity, on the one hand, and the fear on the other hand of what man can do to us, the fear perhaps of war or atomic weapons. Such disquieting reflections may very well be present to our minds. Yet I dare to counsel you not to face the future with dismay or fear. Rather would I have you face it with courage, faith and hope. I would have you do this, not because you are strong. Life is stronger than the strongest. Not because you are wise. Few of us are wise. Not because here and there the clouds are breaking. Clouds that lift may soon return again. Not for any of those earth-born reasons, would I bid you take courage and hope, but rather for this compelling all-sufficing reason, that the Lord Jesus, the all-powerful, all-wise and all-knowing, has given us His own promise, "I will never under any circumstances let you down, I will never never forsake you."

IV

BEGINNINGS

1. WHAT IT MEANS TO BE A CHRISTIAN
(For young men and women)

Nevertheless I live; yet not I, but Christ liveth in me (Gal. ii. 20).

WHAT does it mean to be a Christian? Let us begin by indicating what it does not mean. An Indian for example lumps all who come from the West as Christians to mark them off from those who are Hindus, Buddhists or Mohammedans. That they may be far from being Christian is shown by an observation of a highly-placed Malayan official made to Dr. Stanley Jones, that nearly all the Western Christians he had met were marked by two hatreds, a hatred of religion and pure water. Nor does association with the Christian Church make a man a Christian. It only puts him in the way of being one, but it does not necessarily make him one. Nor does a knowledge of the Bible, and acceptance of the creeds of the Church, lead to this result, if a man does not proceed upon this knowledge and build it into his life. James in his Epistle tells us that even the Devil believes, but obviously not unto salvation. We can go still further and confidently allege that not even living a good life makes a man a Christian. If that were so, then the rich young ruler who had kept all the commandments would have had no need to ask Jesus, "What lack I yet?"; nor would Paul who was blameless as touching the righteousness that was in the law have needed conversion. There are many people who live irreproachable moral lives who are not Christians, and would never dream of calling themselves such. If then contact with a Christian civilisation, the practice of religious ordinances, the holding of correct creedal beliefs, the practice of an exalted morality are false or defective descriptions of what a Christian life is, how can we arrive at the truth of the matter? Can we find an all-inclusive phrase or New Testament text which lights up our perplexity and puts us in the way of a satisfactory answer to our question? Perhaps this Pauline text comes nearer to the truth than any other statement, "I live; yet not I, but Christ liveth in me." The two notes that mark a complete Christian life according to this definition are self-crucifixion and Christ-possessedness.

First then *the death of self*. The "I," the ego no longer lives, but is destroyed. This is Christ's own definition. "If any man would come after me, let him say 'no' to self, take up his own cross of self-renunciation daily, and follow after Me." Jesus is not thinking of self-denial or self-sacrifice in this connection, although doubtless that is implied, the thought in His mind is that of self denied. What He asks is not that self should be repressed, suppressed or disciplined, but completely eliminated, annihilated, crucified, that it should be a doomed, dying, and ultimately a dead, thing. The symbol of the Christian faith is a Cross, and what is the shape of a cross but an "I" with a cancelling line running through it? The ego ceases to count. Its lusts and appetites lose their hold. The old self no longer rules the mind. This tyrant, this greedy vain, ambitious, aggressive self, has ceased to dominate and control the life, another master reigns in its stead.

The second mark of the Christian life *is Christ-centredness*. "Christ liveth in me," says Paul, not simply as one of many influences, but so possessedly as to exclude every egotistic impulse. He alone lives and reigns in me. The origin of the word Christian is significant in this connection. The followers of Christ at the beginning called themselves not Christians but "disciples," "believers," "witnesses," "saints." They received that name first at Antioch, and it was really a nickname which the pagans coined to express their sense of the singularity of their witness. They were palpably a peculiar people, with an outlook, an ethos, a manner of speech and behaviour which were quite new and strange in Antioch. So different were they from the pagans around them, that some one has described the contrast as resembling a Biblical quotation in a political speech. They lived pure, loving, selfless lives in an environment that reeked with jealousies, lasciviousness and selfish ambition. Their lives gravitated round a centre other than self, and when they studied them closely as they were bound to do, it was discovered that all their thought and speech and interest centred on One whom they called Christos. So they nicknamed them the Christians, the men in whom Christ lived and reigned.

And what the men of Antioch observed, Paul experienced and expressed. "I live; yet not I, but Christ liveth in me." Paul found in Christ the perfect equation for life. In Philip. i. 21 he writes, "Life means Christ to me," but he might equally have written, "Christ means life to me." His life swung round Christ, as planets round a central sun. The life he lived in the flesh he lived in the faith of the son of God. It was a life Christ-originated, Christ-sustained, Christ-directed and Christ-destined. Christ was the fountain, the support, the purpose and the goal of his earthly life. He was not but in Christ. Paul was merely the body of Christ. He was Christ's bond-slave, wholly at His disposal, His, both in life and death. Matheson has summed up the meaning of being a Christian in these familiar words. "I lay in dust life's glory dead, and from the ground there blossoms red, life that shall endless be."

That such a state of Christ-possession is possible is easily demonstrated. The poet speaks about "the wonder that is in the heart." And truly the heart has a marvellous capacity for expansiveness and hospitality. Filth can go into the heart till it becomes a cesspool, as Jesus reminds us in Mark vii. 21, and Paul in Romans i. But other things can go in also, things lovely, true, pure and of good report —sustaining ideas, gleaming ideals, sacrificial loves, the vision of seas, mountains, stars, infinitudes, kingdoms. "The kingdom of God is within you," said Jesus. All these things can go into the heart, and here is another thing that can go there also—people. A man once stood beside an open grave into which were laid the mortal remains of his beloved wife. He lingered long there, weeping salt bitter tears. Then a friend gently touched his arm and said softly, "Come away, my friend, it were better so." Dazed with grief, he turned away, and, as he did so, he said passionately, "I thank God for the day that that good woman came into my life." Many of us have good reason to thank God for the day that that God-man came into our lives. "This is a great mystery," writes Paul in his Colossian epistle, "hid from all generations, that has now been revealed to His people: to whom it was His will to make known how vast a wealth of glory for the Gentile world is implied in this truth—the truth that 'Christ is in you, the hope of glory' " (Weymouth). When Christ lives and reigns in our hearts we begin to know what it means to be a Christian.

This definition helps to clear up most of the mis-understandings and perplexities which the practice of the Christian life raises, and simplifies the whole issue. Many young Christians are puzzled as to the right Christian re-action to certain dubious choices offered them by the world. They find a difficulty in knowing where they should draw the line. Should they mix in the world, share in its amusements, recreations and secular interests? Should they say "No" to the alluring enticements of the flesh? Should they dance, play cards, go to the theatre, etc.? Should they engage their strength simply in avoiding faults? Should they lay the axe to the root of the tree, cut adrift from everything compromising and indulge in denunciation of what seems to them to be evil? These problems are legion, and must be faced and met, as they arise. It will help, however, if we remember that the Christian life is not elimination, negation, prohibition nor denunciation but, habitation. It is Christ in us. And if Christ is in us, we have a Monitor within which keeps us right. We have the spirit of the living Christ that guides us into all truth. In any given situation we ought to know what to do, if we consult the living Presence within. For Christ speaks to every wayfaring man, and if we listen to Him He will say to us clearly, "This is the way, walk ye in it." Each must be persuaded in his own mind by the pressure of the directing presence within.

Once again, if Christ lives within us, we have a complete safeguard against the assaults of temptation. Samuel Rutherford in one of his letters urges a young convert to prayer and watchfulness against the sins of youth, "for I know that missive letters go between the Devil and young blood. Satan hath a friend at court in the heart of youth, and their pride, luxury, hate, revenge, forgetfulness of God are hired as his agents." Many are the defences offered against temptation. We are urged especially to defend the fortress of the soul by filling it with high ideals. Above the doorway of a schoolmaster's house in Paris are written the words, "Molière lives here. Shakespeare lives here. Dante lives here." Happy the man whose mind is saturated with the master thoughts of the master spirits of the ages. But thrice armed is the man whose heart glows with the love of Jesus, whose affections are set on things above, whose mind is inspired with heavenly thoughts, and whose will is reinforced by divine energy. When the Hugenots were besieged at St. Quentin, the Spaniards shot an arrow into the market place, carrying a scornful demand for surrender. Coligny, the commander of the Hugenots shot back the paper, adding only two words, "Regem habemus." "We have a King." Young blood will scornfully reply to the Devil's missives, "We have a King who contests your rule, and He lives and reigns within us." "Put ye on the Lord Jesus Christ, and make no provision for the flesh to fulfil the lusts thereof."

One aspect of this question which often puzzles and discourages young people should be mentioned before we close. It is the bewildering discrepancy in the quality of life shown by those who equally claim to be Christ's followers. Christians are by no means equal in the impressiveness of their witness. There are bad, indifferent, good and superlatively good Christians. There are those whose lives are scarcely to be distinguished from rank worldings, and others who stand out from their fellows with the brightness of a light shining in a dark place. What is it that determines the difference? Surely it is determined by the place they give to Christ or self in their lives. Milton discloses the secret in these sonorous words. "I conceive myself to be not as my own person, but as a man incorporated into the truth of which I am persuaded." Our quality of life depends on the richness of our implantations. "Abide in me, and I in you. As the branch cannot bear fruit of itself, except it abide in the Vine; no more can ye, except ye abide in Me." Croce, the Italian philosopher, defined beauty as "successful expression" and the really beautiful Christian life is one in which Christ successfully expresses Himself. Saintliness is just successful Christ-expression. The achievement of such a lovely life, what Paul calls "the prize of our high calling," is a slow and painful process, and we must not easily be discouraged. The self life is a rebellious and stubborn tyrant, who is reluctant to yield up the sceptre of his rule even to the Lordship of Christ. In our own strength we cannot discrown the self. We can only do so, as we daily and hourly take up our cross of self-renunciation, follow Christ and allow Him in all ways of obedience, to work in us both to will and do of His good pleasure. When we reach the point when we can say to Christ, "none of self and all of Thee," we have attained to successful Christ-expression.

The story is told of a German prince that he had a passionate desire to purchase a Cremona violin. He offered an exorbitant sum for its purchase. For months he failed to elicit any response to his advertisement. Then one day an old man came to the door of his castle, carrying a violin in a shabby case. The servants would have turned him away from the door, but he prevailed on them at last to carry this cryptic message to their master, "Tell him, that all heaven's music is knocking at his door." When this message was delivered, the Prince asked the man to be admitted. When he entered his presence he took the violin

from its case, swept the chords with his fingers, and drew
forth such ravishing music, that the prince was intoxicated. He offered any sum for the violin. But the old man
stated his conditions. "This violin can only be purchased
on one condition, that I stay as a guest in your place, and
none will ever play it except myself." To be a complete
Christian is to admit Christ into our hearts as perpetual
Guest, to ask Him to evoke with the magic of His touch
all the chords of our life, to draw forth into successful
expression all the music that is in us, and allow no one
but Himself to do so.

2. THE CALL OF THE MASTER
(*For the uncommitted*)

Martha called Mary her sister secretly, saying, "The Master is come and
calleth for thee" (John xi. 28).

"The Master is come, and calleth for thee." That was
the good news that Martha conveyed to her sister Mary.
It was a matter for profound regret that He hadn't come
a little sooner. "If Thou had'st been here, my brother
had not died." Even yet the situation was not beyond the
reach of the Master's control. "I know that, even now,
whatsoever Thou wilt ask of God, God will grant it."
When the Master comes the most desperate situations can
be retrieved, the impossible becomes possible, and every
hopeless outlook big with promise. This announcement of
Martha is a gospel for to-day. Let us examine more closely
its implications.

That the Master is come is good news indeed, *because
we all need a Master*. We need some controlling power to
keep under leash our unbridled passions and appetites,
and belt them to useful ends. The first essential for power
of any kind is rigid control. All high-powered machinery
has its controls—the aeroplane its joy-stick, the motor-car
its gears, the locomotive its brakes. Even more urgently
does the delicate, complicated, high-geared machinery of

human nature demand its controls. We need a Master, "who from vain temptations dost set free, and calm'st the weary strife of frail mortality." The Old Testament prototype of physical strength was Samson, sinewy in limb and muscle, tempestuous in temperament, but weak in control of his powers. His tragedy was that he lived a masterless life, where he badly needed a Master. In the end Milton puts into his lips the tragic consequences of an uncontrolled life:

> I, like a foolish pilot, have shipwrecked
> My vessel trusted to me from above
> Gloriously rigged.

We boast proudly that we are masters in our own household, but Jesus, with much greater perspicacity, says that "a man's foes are they of his own household." Human nature without adequate controls is in a state of perpetual siege. Civil war rages in its members. "The flesh lusteth against the spirit, and the spirit against the flesh." Without control we are like a team of wild horses stampeding in opposite directions at one and the same time: like a ship's crew in mutiny against its captain: like the members of an orchestra playing from different musical scores: like an army that disobeys orders and ignores king's regulations. We need a strong hand on the reins, a captain on the bridge, a maestro who can wield a baton, a commander who enforces obedience.

Nations as well as individuals need a Master. The absence of a Master, or at any rate the failure to honour one, is the root cause of the trouble in the world to-day. In many respects we are less fortunately situated than those living in the Middle Ages. Spite of the defects that marred their economy, the people of that time had at least universal standards everywhere acknowledged if not obeyed. There was a universal Church—the Catholic universal philosophy—the Scholastic; a universal law— the Roman; a universal language—the Latin; a universal art—the Gothic; a universal ethic—the Christian; a universal code of manners—chivalry. That has all gone.

To-day there is no King in Israel. There is no universally recognised standard of morality which all alike respect, no common rule of action which all agree to follow, no supreme authority which commands universal allegiance. Each nation does that which is expedient in its own eyes. Each consults merely its own self-interest, and as the interests of each clash with the other, the net result is confusion worse confounded. How is it possible to secure world-order and peace under such prevailing anarchic conditions? We need to-day beyond everything else a Master to deliver us from the tyranny of sectionalism and daemonism, and to make the life of the world one-directional. The late Dr. Kelman on one occasion was travelling across the Atlantic to America. On board his vessel were three of the leading statesmen of the world. One night their talk turned on world politics, and on the appalling confusion that existed in world affairs. Dr. Kelman asked these three men if they could offer any solution for this tragic state of things. One of them said, "What is wanted is a world-Emperor." "Yes," said Dr. Kelman, "but where is such a Person to be found?" "He already exists," was the quiet reply, "and His name is Jesus Christ." The nations need a Master.

Not only do we need a Master, but *we desire a Master*. Wordsworth has given classical expression to this dominant desire in his "Ode to Duty."

> Me this unchartered freedom tires
> I feel the weight of chance-desires;
> My hopes no more must change their name,
> I long for a repose that ever is the same.

That may not seem so on the surface, but when we know our need, "in the quietness of thought" as Wordsworth puts it, "I supplicate for thy control." This runs true to human nature. Even boys and girls at school appreciate a master who rules with a firm hand. The only happy homes in the land are those where a wise and loving discipline rules. Soldiers in the ranks may grouse at the austerities of military training, but they infinitely prefer an iron discipline to laxity and indirection. Someone has said that "a man's real difficulties begin when he is free to do what he likes." The Prodigal Son was in this condition, but in the end he preferred the lot of one of the hired servants in his Father's house to the free life of "the far country." The children of Israel in Samuel's day grew weary of an invisible monarchy, and demanded from him a visible king who would lead them to battle, and lay down rules for common social action. We desire a Master. One of the commonest fallacies men cherish is, that "a man's life consisteth in the abundance of the things he possesseth." Precisely the opposite is the truth. His true life consists, not in the things he possesses, but in the things that possess *him*. It is not the things that belong to us that set the bells of our nature ringing, but the things to which we belong—the attachments that bind us, the loves that grip us, the interests that govern us, the appreciations which inflame us, the aspirations which lift us, the causes we serve which command our allegiance, and engage all our powers.

Once we grasp this truth we hold the key to much that is perplexing in the life of our age. It explains among other things the rise of dictatorships and the emergence of the Totalitarian State. It may seem inexplicable that masses of people and nations are prepared to sell the pass of liberty and give a sacrificial devotion to men of doubtful antecedents and questionable character, till we remember the vacuum created by the post-war world. This passionate and blind obedience is the protest of the soul against a masterless world. Men desire and must possess a Master. They must march under some banner. They must have some flag to serve. And if they fail to find good leaders, they will follow bad leaders, for bad leadership is better than none at all. The popularity of the Führer principle, the rise to autocratic power of unscrupulous dictators, is born of the bankruptcy of Democracy to furnish convincing and effective leadership, as well as of the failure of the Christian Church to establish the claim of Christ to rule as Master over men and nations.

It is time to remind ourselves that, as we need and desire a Master, *we do, in point of fact, possess one.* "The Master *is* come." He came two thousand years ago to this earth, and graced it with His blessed Presence. He moved in and out amongst us, full of grace and truth, but also of authority. He was incontestably the Master then, the Master of men, events, situations, circumstances, relationships. He was Master of the realm of the Absolute, breathing that rarified air as if it were His native element.

He has given us the only thought of God that can stand the strain of life, has given to men the assurance of God's presence, and transmitted to the world His gifts of pardon, peace and power. He is Master in the realm of human speech. His words—so simple, colourful, significant, vital, universal—are a miracle of creative power. "Never man spake like this Man." His words are as relevant to the needs of to-day as when uttered on the Galilean hills; and they will remain when Heaven and earth have passed away. He was the Master of men, calling to Himself those whom He would, binding them in a fellowship that death itself could not destroy, and securing from them the service of a cause which demanded the utmost in sacrifice and executive efficiency. He was Master in the realm of psychology. He read the human heart like an open book. Did not Nathaniel exclaim wonderingly, "How knowest Thou me?" And did not the woman of Samaria instance His penetration as evidence of His Messiahship. "Come, see a Man who told me all things that ever I did." He knew what was in man, the best as well as the worst. Who but the Master would have seen in a greedy tax-gatherer a capacity for liberality as romantic as Abraham's, in the inconstant Peter, the rock on which His Church would be built, or in the soiled Magdalene the vision of a "King's daughter, all-glorious within." If it is the authentic mark of the Leader that he detects and draws out the hidden possibilities of human nature, then Jesus was the world's greatest Leader. He was Master also in the realm of disease. He sent forth His word and healed all in need of healing. Even the tassel of His robe had healing virtue in it. It was a Roman centurion who spotted that He had the control of supernatural agencies which did His bidding more swiftly and effectively than the Roman legions obeyed his own orders. He had only to speak the word of healing and swift-winged ministrants executed His orders. There was no disease, however malignant, which did not yield to His masterly touch. Even the dark world of the demons stubbornly and reluctantly yielded up their authority at His word. "We know Thee, who Thou art, Thou Holy One of Israel," they cried in terror. He was Master in the realm of Nature too. Even its rigid and uniform laws were plastic to His touch. He spoke to the stormy sea of Galilee, as if it were a wild beast, saying "Be muzzled!" and there was a great calm. When He turned water into wine, "the conscious water saw its Lord and blushed." Even death itself could not hold its prey in its cold clutch when its sovereign Lord drew near. Martha was never more right than when she surmised, that Jesus was Lord of death as well as of life. Jesus was Master then, and He is Master now. On His head to-day are many crowns. All authority in Heaven and earth has been delegated to Him. He sits at God's right hand as King for ever. By his spirit He still exercises authority over all the earth. He is willing and eager to be Master of our nature, our powers, our lot, our character and our destiny. Will we have this Man to rule over us?

Dr. Leslie Weatherhead tells a story about a cowboy from the Wild West, who happened to find himself in Church on Palm Sunday. The preacher read and spoke of Christ's entry into Jerusalem. He heard for the first time the story of Christ riding on an unbroken colt, and holding the beast in such a way that it rode on calmly and undisturbed, although multitudes were shouting in its ears, and still more irritatingly waving palm branches before its eyes. The cowboy's only comment was, "What wonderful hands He must have had!" When we reflect on the mulishness of our nature, its stubborness and obstinacy, when we think of its wildness and indiscipline, its unregulated passions and appetites, and then remember that Christ can break our pride, subdue our appetites, expel the demons within, and make us self-controlled and serviceable persons, we can only say, "What wonderful hands He must have!" And if to this we add His power to integrate, enrich and fulfil our nature, then with hushed and adoring awe we whisper to our souls "The Master indeed has come."

Finally we possess a *Master who seeks to possess us.*

His message He has broadcast to the whole world, but His call He addresses intimately and personally to each individual." The Master is come and calleth *for thee.*" Let us ask ourselves in all seriousness what is the nature of the response we are making to that call. Do we recognise Him as the one and only Master of human life? Do we feel about Him what the Earl of Kent felt about another in Shakespeare's play, "There is that in thee which I would fain call Master"? And do we feel that, as He has earned the right to rule over us, we ought to obey His call? Are we willing now to sanctify Christ as Lord in our hearts? Are we prepared to accept His rule, to submit to His yoke, to trust in Him as our Saviour, and follow Him as our Leader?

Recently, when working in Melbourne, I picked up one of their leading newspapers, *The Age,* and was struck by the substance and form of one of its leading articles. I learned afterwards that it was written by the Baptist octogenarian, Dr. Boreham. The article was all about the Australian way of life. It quoted an observation of Priestley that, after reading several books on Australia for purposes of review, he "laid them aside with a shudder." Apparently the English novelist did not relish the Australian way of life. And then the writer goes on to say, that the Australian way of life is just what the Australian citizen is. Then he added significantly, "the Australian citizen is the kind of person that his Master has made him." Like Master, like subject. That goes for any country in the world as well as Australia. No question then can be more pertinent than this. At what shrine are the citizens of our country worshipping? To whom or what are we giving our dominant allegiance? That is our real Master in every instance. Let me ask then, what God we are serving? Is it the fickle goddess of Chance, what the Greeks called Tyche, or Pluto the God of Wealth, or Bacchus the God of Drink or Pan the God of Pleasure, or Baal the God of Agriculture, or Venus the Goddess of Lust? The Gods we worship will in every case fashion our tastes, mould our character, and shape our destiny. My urgent plea is that we should recognise the claims of Christ, on whose shoulders alone the government of our lives is fit to rest. I would eagerly covet for you all that you make the right choice, enlist under the right flag, and acknowledge the right Master. And as Jesus, the Master, has come, and is still coming, and calling each of us home to Himself, my prayer now is, that we respond to His call with something of the eager alacrity of Mary, of whom it is written that, as soon as Martha told her that the Master had come and was calling for her, "she arose quickly and came to Him."

3. HOW TO BEGIN TO BE A CHRISTIAN
(For those taking the first steps in the Christian life)

Lord, what wilt Thou have me to do? (Acts ix. 6).

Having just considered the question of what it means to be a Christian there may be those whose interest is sufficiently aroused as to create in them the desire to live this life. They are uncertain, however, about the first steps, and like Paul are asking, "Lord, what wilt Thou have me to do?" Beginnings are always important and usually difficult. It takes twice the expenditure of engine-power in an aeroplane to make a clean get-away as to continue airborne. It takes a mighty effort to cut clear from the gravitation of earth and be fairly launched on our heavenly career. My aim here is to offer a few simple elementary principles which will help earnest enquirers to make the necessary initial effort.

The *first* necessary step to take is to *consider* Christ. This is a sound New Testament maxim. Take a good look at the Lord Jesus. Keep looking at Him. Hold Him steadily before your minds. Isaac Newton was once asked what he did when confronted with a difficult problem in physics. His answer was, "I keep it before me." Keep Christ before you—His words, deeds, sacrifice, example, spirit, His impressive and engaging Personality. It must be sun-clear to you, that if the picture of Jesus is never before you, He can mean to you less than nothing at all. So as a beginning consider Christ. Consider Christ, not Christians. We are all tempted to judge Christ by His followers, and leave the matter there. That is, however, a precarious approach to the Christian life, as so many of His representatives offer only a wrong or defective image of His beauty. When the High Priest asked Jesus of His disciples, He kept a stony silence. He had no plea for the moment to offer for the men who had just forsaken Him and fled. But even when the type we examine does in some fair measure reflect the loveliness of Christ, it still falls far short of Christ's perfection. I remember once being in the Louvre in Paris, where Leonardo's great masterpiece is on view, "La Gioconda." Round it were grouped half a dozen painters, busily engaged in reproducing the original painting. They were all competent reproductions, but even to my inexperienced eye, they fell far short of the original. They lacked what Joshua Reynolds called "just that", that inner spark of life, that sureness of touch which was the Master's own secret. Consider the Original not the copy: Christ Himself, not the Christian. Again, consider Christ, not His Church. The Church is important, nay indispensable, because it is the medium for the expression of Christ's spirit, and the instrument for the extension of His Kingdom on earth. But the institution has not the same value as its Founder. It is the garment of Christ, but the garment is often spotted and stained. It is the Bride, but she has often proved herself to be weak and faithless. She is His Body, but it has frequently been wrinkled and spotted. "I could stand Christ," said Swinburne foolishly and cynically, "did He not come trailing His leprous Bride with Him." The Church has all the faults belonging to an institution partly of the earth, and staffed by sinful fallen mortals. So though I love the Church and honour her for her Founder's sake as well as for her work's sake, my first counsel to you is to concentrate your thoughts for the moment neither on Christians nor on the Church but on Christ Himself. Consider Christ. He is worth considering. On any account, He is without question the most impressive Personality that has ever crossed the stage of history. Fortunately for us the materials for considering Him are amply sufficient. They are to be found in the Four Gospels which are accessible to all, and can be purchased for a few pence. Read, ponder and inwardly digest them, and especially, to begin with, the Gospel of Mark. I suppose most of you go to the "movies," to look at the living features of actors and actresses, representing the great drama of life. Yet here in the Gospels are reproduced the lineaments of Him who wrought out the most stupendous drama of history, moving pictures which grip the heart and fire the imagination, pictures that are also true, representing the holy living and sacrificial dying of the Son of God as well as His glorious triumph over sin and death. Consider Him who "is the lonely greatness of the world."

When Abraham Lincoln met his tragic death, a long funeral procession followed his remains through the streets of Boston, which were lined with silent mournful spectators. Among the spectators was a poor negro woman with her little boy by her side. As the cortege slowly passed the spot where she stood, she was observed to lift her boy on to her shoulders and say, "Take a long look at him, honey, he died for you." Take a long look at Christ. He lived, died, and rose again for you. Among the multiplicity of things that are engaging your interest, do not neglect to consider the significance for you of the Christ of history.

My *second* point is that you should not only consider

Him but *receive* Him. Jesus can do nothing for any of us till we receive Him into our hearts. Reception is a condition of all influence. A public speaker or performer is powerless, if his audience is resolutely set against Him. A friend of mine, in the dramatic line, confessed to me that she was very nervous about a certain public appearance she had to make. She was entertaining a group of soldiers who were critical of the kind of programme served up to them. From the bitterness of past experience she knew that, if they didn't like you, they would, as she put it, "give you the bird." I can conceive no torture more exquisite than the lot of a sensitive professional comedian whose best quips are greeted in stony silence or with howls of derision. Every preacher of the living word knows that his effectiveness depends as much on the sensitiveness of his hearers' reception as on the quality of his message, A ministerial friend of mine once advertised as his evening subject "the secret of successful preaching." As the sequel proved, success depended not so much on the skilful technique of the preacher, his oratorical power, his persuasive gifts, nor even on the quality of the seed he was sowing as on the nature of the soil into which it fell. Jesus Himself has countersigned this truth in the parable of the Sower, or as I prefer to call it, the parable of the four soils. Not even the heavenly Sower could get satisfactory results from thin, hard or rank soil. "A good and honest heart" is an essential condition for the hundredfold harvest. And the pre-requisite condition for fruitful preaching of the word is even more essential for the effectual influence of the Word Incarnate in our lives. A great surgeon who had entered into a saving experience of Christ gave it as his deliberate and considered judgement that Christianity was pure receptivity. This hospitable reception of Christ and His claims is what Jesus asks, expects, and demands from us. This is the measure of our responsibility. But we must give it to Him voluntarily, for He refuses to extort it from us forcibly. He refuses to cross the sacred threshold of our being unless we invite Him. A few years ago young King Edward came to Glasgow to take part in the ceremony of launching a ship. He took the opportunity, while there, of acquiring first-hand knowledge of the city's social conditions. He climbed, along with members of his staff, a block of buildings at Anderston Cross, till he arrived at the humble abode of a widow woman who lived all alone. Knocking courteously at the door (for not even a king may invade the sanctity of a private home), he was greeted by a voice within, "who's there?" To her amazement the woman received the reply. "Your king is here. May I come in?" The Lord Jesus, King of Kings, knocks at the door of our hearts and says, "Your King is here. May I come in?" Will you receive Him? You receive other things—news, views, ideas, ideals, persons, parsons. Will you refuse to receive the highest, this divinest Guest, this Friend of Friends? Open the door now and receive Him gladly into your hearts.

And the *last* thing to do is not only to consider and to receive Him, but *to trust Him*. Commit your lives wholly to His keeping. That is what faith mainly, although not wholly, means in the New Testament. In the words of the Shorter Catechism, "Faith is a saving grace whereby we receive and rest upon Christ alone for salvation, as it is freely offered to us in the Gospel." In asking you then to make this act of self-committal to Christ I am not making any new or strange demand on you. A friend of mine some time ago got into the London-Glasgow train, and opposite to him sat a bright little boy of ten years, travelling all alone. He asked him where he was going, and he told him he was going to Crewe. "That's a long distance for a little chap like you to travel all alone." "Not so far," he replied. "Aren't you afraid to go all that distance alone?" was his next question. "Oh no," said the boy, "you see, my father is the engine-driver." He was trusting his father to see him through. That is what we all do consciously or unconsciously. When we plough the fields and scatter the seed we are trusting the ground to bring forth bountifully of itself, when we go forth to our work till the evening, we are relying on the constancy of Nature's laws, or rather let us say, we are trusting to our Father to implement His promises. Trust is really the key to life. The whole business world is run on a basis of trust. It is the life blood of friendship. We all take each other on trust. It is the basis of all international treaties and the bond by which society holds together. There is nothing new in the demand that we put our trust in the Invisible Christ.

The only proviso we make, when we commit ourselves, is that the object or person we trust be trustworthy. Well, isn't Christ worthy of all our trust? By His words and deeds and sufferings for the human race He has established an incontestable claim to our trust. Some time ago I met a fellow-traveller on a bus who turned out to be a missionary to deep-sea fishermen. A part of his mission lay amongst deep-sea divers. He told me an interesting thing about them. He said that when they went down into deep waters their only concern was that the man on the surface who held the life-lines should be a man who *himself had gone down into the deep*. Well hasn't the Lord Jesus descended into Hades for us, gone down deeper than the lowest deeps of human need? Has He not endured the Cross for us, despising its shame, paid the uttermost price to establish His credentials? The late Wm. Arnot tells of a poor honest woman in his parish in Glasgow who had got into debt through no fault of her own. Hearing of her plight, he collected sufficient money to meet all her obligations. One day he called in person, taking with him the money he had collected. When he knocked at her door to deliver it up he received no answer. Calling the following day she reluctantly opened the door. When he explained that he had called the previous day, she told him she had heard the knock, but she hadn't opened the door, because she was afraid that it was the rent-collector. When he told her that he had brought her the money to pay all her debts, she burst into tears, and said, "How terrible to think that I locked the door against my deliverer." We often treat in the same fashion the Saviour who comes to pay our debts, and set us free. Is He not worthy of all our trust? Has He not proved again and yet again His trustworthiness? There is no conceivable situation in our lives which we may not safely trust Him to see us through. You needn't be afraid that if you commit yourselves wholly to Him you will bring discredit on His name and cause by your weakness and failure. You can trust Him to keep from falling the life He has ransomed from the pit. You needn't be afraid that His power will fail you when comes your evil day. "It is with no weak Christ you have to do," said Paul, "but with the Christ of power." He is able and willing to keep that which is committed to Him. He is able to do in us, for us, through us exceeding abundantly above all that we can ask or think. Now unto Him who is able to keep us from falling and present us at last faultless before His Presence with exultant joy, be ascribed all praise and glory, now and for evermore.

4. THE GREAT DISCOVERY
(*For Witness Week*)

We have found Him (John i. 45).

"We have found Him." That is something that should be deeply pondered. In an age of problems it is satisfactory to find solutions. In periods of restless questionings there is always an audience for those who can proclaim certainties. And when the issues raised are fundamental, and are concerned with our total way of life, the knowledge that we have found Him who is the Way, the Truth, and the Life is good news indeed. Such was the burden of the message of Philip to Nathaniel. "We have found," he said, "the answer to Israel's hope and expectation"; nay, he might have added, "We have found the answer to all life's questionings, the goal of our heart's desire, the key that unlocks the gates of everlasting life." It will be our purpose now to explore more fully the significance of this discovery.

To begin with, to find Jesus is always *a personal discovery*. It is the discovery of a Person by persons. It has all the immediacy, intimacy and reciprocity of a personal encounter. It is an I-Thou relationship. It is two persons meeting and mingling their lives. There are those with deep religious instincts who yet never reach this level of reality. They have read much about Jesus, heard much of Him, been interested in Him, know a lot about Him, but are strangers to the knowledge of Christ Himself. The Christian religion is to them a body of doctrine, a code of morals, a standard of values, a way of looking at, and handling life. Such an attitude is good enough so far as it goes, but it remains sub-Christian because it doesn't go far enough. The real thing is a discovery. And the discovery is that Jesus is not dead but alive, not a figure of history but a living Contemporary, who meets us in the ways of modern life, and seeks to have intimately personal dealings with us. Being essentially a discovery, it has all the surprise, romance and frequently the unexpectedness which the personal introduces into life. It is like the experience of falling in love, an old old story to many now, but always to those who experience it for the first time, strange, exquisite and incredible. G. Meredith once encountered a youth who had found Christ, and he babbled to him endlessly of his new experience. When someone asked him if he wasn't bored with these gushing effusions, he answered quietly, "No, I never tire of sunrises." This is the very metaphor Paul uses to describe his discovery of Jesus. It was like the falling of scales from the eyes, and the letting in of a great light. In one beautiful passage in 2 Corinthians he likens this experience of discovery to the change that took place in the dark primeval world when light first emerged. "God, who commanded the light to shine out of the darkness, hath shined in our hearts, to give the light of the knowledge of the glory of God in the face of Jesus Christ."

It follows from this, that to find Christ *is a very precious discovery*. This is par excellence the age of discovery. Psychology, exploring the contents of human personality, is discovering unsuspected forces and energies there which, harnessed and directed aright, will enormously increase human efficiency. Physicists are investigating the properties of matter, and belting its enormous powers to the uses of man. Medical science is tracking down with increasing success the roots of malignant disease, and applying more enlightened therapeutic methods to their cure. These are important discoveries which are easing the burden of toil and pain, and adding to our comfort, efficiency and length of days.

Yet there is one discovery more important than all these, which is largely neglected and unused: the discovery, namely, that very near to us is an unrecognised Ally who is able to do for us and in us "exceeding abundantly above all we can ask or think." When Sir James Simpson was asked what his most important discovery was, he replied, "The discovery that I have a Saviour." Jesus Himself unfailingly stressed His importance for human life. "Without Me," He said, "you can do nothing," that is, nothing that is spiritually significant. In one parable He said that the discovery of Him was like a man finding "hid treasure in a field." One moment he was a poor man, the next rich beyond the dreams of avarice. In another parable He says that it is like a pearl merchant finding the Queen Pearl at the end of a long quest, a gem, so to speak, which includes, sums up and overtops the worth of all the lesser jewels put together. In another place He claims that He is living Bread, not chocolate, nor confection, nor some luxurious addendum to life, but the staff of life itself, something in the absence of which a man cannot be said to live at all. This runs true to experience. Jesus is so precious that He is life itself and something more, as John writes in his Gospel. Paul who had discovered Jesus for himself, and knew Him intimately and possessively, claimed that Jesus was the perfect equation for life. "Life means Christ to me." So great was the worth of this discovery in this man's eyes, that he judged that his pre-Christian life, rich though it was, full of engaging interests, solid achievements and future promise, that same life, now that Jesus met him and changed him, seemed to him to be a worthless thing, a rotting, nay, a malodorous thing. "For Christ's sake I have learned to count my former gains a loss. Indeed I count anything a loss compared to the supreme value of knowing Christ Jesus my Lord"

(Moffatt). F. W. Myers, voicing Paul's experience, as well as that of all who have made this precious discovery writes,

> Who that one moment hath the least descried Him,
>   Dimly and faintly, hidden and afar,
> Doth not despise all excellence beside Him,
>   Pleasures and powers that are not, and that are?

Again, this discovery *is a life-changing discovery.*

Its chief effect is its beneficient action on human character. When we discover Jesus we discover ourselves, when we know Him we know our own hearts, when He controls us, we learn to control our nature. This is not true of any other kind of discovery. The discoveries in the realm of the applied sciences leave character unaffected. They are good, bad or indifferent, according to the use made of them. Aeroplanes may carry lethal weapons or hospital equipment, ships munitions or merchandise, the printing press issue pornographic or sacred literature, the radio sponsor mass lying or Gospel propaganda. Every discovery made by man may be a savour of life-unto-life or of death-unto-death. But the discovery of Jesus does good, always good, and nothing but good. When Jesus is intimately known, when He lives, loves and reigns in our hearts, the wilderness within begins to rejoice and blossom as the rose. We become partakers of the divine nature. The pardon, peace, power and poise of the divine life possess us. We are born anew of the Spirit and are translated out of the realm of darkness into light, out of bondage into the glorious liberty of the children of God. To find Jesus is to find ourselves in another world, where the supernatural forces of the spiritual world operate within us, and recreate our whole being. On one occasion an unknown stranger came to Freiburg in South Germany. He went to visit the Cathedral with a view to playing on its famous organ. He courteously asked the verger for this privilege, but he stoutly refused. "No one," he said, "is allowed to play on that organ without the consent of the organist." But the stranger pleaded so persuasively that he finally yielded to his solicitation, and allowed him to play for a few moments. As the stranger took his seat at the organ and began to play a miracle took place. Through fretted arch and aisle throbbed and sobbed rich harmonies, now swelling into triumph and anon dying away into soft cadences, "linked sweetness long drawn out." Never had the old verger heard such a cascade of rich melodies issuing from his loved organ. His eyes filled with tears, and deeply moved he asked the stranger, "Who are you? What is your name?" "My name," he said, "is Mendelssohn." When we find Jesus, we find the only Master who knows how to bring out of us the best that is in us. He brings harmony into the discords of our nature. He sounds notes in us whose very existence we never suspected—love-notes, tremolo-notes, fortissimo-notes. And as we reflect on the difference He makes to our lives, the sweetness and purity He brings, the enrichment and extension of our powers, we feel disposed to say to Him what this verger said to the distinguished musician, "How dreadful to think that I almost refused to allow you to play on my organ."

Once more, the discovery of Jesus *is a self-publishing discovery*. It betrays its presence by its effects. It manifests itself by its witness. A Christian life is an epistle of God read and known of all men. Emerson somewhere writes, "The universe proclaims itself by a merciless publicity." The Christ-found life declares itself by its manifestations. It is like a city set on an hill which cannot be hid. This is not true of men who make other forms of discovery. There is no essential relation between the discoverer and the thing discovered. A man might engage in philosophical speculation and his life bear no trace of it. A man is not necessarily a great character because he is a great scientist. When the electric cable was being laid down in Glasgow for the first time, Lord Kelvin worked in the trench in dungarees like an ordinary labourer. A young student passing by looked at him superciliously and said, "Hallo old boy, what do you know about electricity?" The great authority looked at him with solemn eyes and said drily, "Not very much I am afraid." You couldn't tell that

Kelvin was the world's greatest expert on electricity by looking at him. We ought however to be able to spot a Christian by looking at him. He should carry his credentials in his face. When Phillips Brooks, the great American preacher, walked down the streets of Boston, an American newspaper reported, "It was a dark gloomy day, but Phillips Brooks walked down the street, and the sun shone through." A man who has found Jesus must publish the discovery in his life, in his attitude to others, in the way he does his work and bears his trials. In third John we find this striking phrase. "Everybody testifies to Demetrius and *so does the Truth itself.*" It shines in its own light. "Ye are light in the Lord," said Paul, and nothing is so intrusive and self-revealing as light. A man who has made the great discovery should attest it in everything he does and says and is. We ought to know a preacher who has found Jesus by his accent of assurance. There should be a difference between a soloist singing a sacred piece to display his voice and one who is singing the Redeemer's praises. On one occasion a banquet was held in a church hall, to which a famous actor was invited. He was asked to read the Shepherd Psalm. He read it with exquisitely modulated voice and received a round of applause. He himself then asked that the oldest member of the Congregation should read the same Psalm. An aged saint read it in a thin and broken voice, and a deep hush fell on the audience. There was no applause when he finished but instead a deep and reverent silence. "You see the difference," said the actor, "between him and me. I know the Psalm, but he knows the Shepherd."

Finally the discovery of Jesus *is one that is open and accessible to all.* That is its peculiar and welcome distinction. Discovery in the geographical field, or in the realm of science or philosophy is reserved for the exceptionally gifted and the highly trained. Even so only the violent can take that kingdom by force. Resoluteness there is as important as brains. Discovery in the realm of physical nature for example is an exacting and costly business. Nature does not yield up her treasures readily or easily.

They have to be filched from her by direct and sustained assault. Only slowly and partially does she open her jealously guarded doors. Read the biography of Madame Curie, if you would know the truth of this matter. She toiled like a galley slave, experimented endlessly, endured one sickening disappointment after another, suffered terribly in her health, before she succeeded in isolating the element of radium, and so wresting her prize from Nature's reluctant grasp.

In the realm of grace, however, God deals far otherwise with us than in the realm of natural law. The veil of God's face is rent by Christ from the top to the bottom. His "never failing treasury, filled with boundless stores of grace," is in Christ made free of all. Jesus Himself is not hid that He cannot be known. Our religion is not a "mystery" religion, For Jesus is the frankness of God, His open face. And the discovery of Him is not only open but accessible to all. It does not depend on our spiritual fitness. It is not here as with the great ethnic faiths where spiritual discovery and communion with God depend on preparatory disciplines, ceremonial rites, legal observances, lustration baths and such like. All the fitness that Jesus requires of us is to feel our need of Him. Any one can find Him who is in earnest in this matter. He is accessible to all, where we are, and as we are. Nay, He is at great pains to make Himself accessible. That is why He became man, and wore the garb of our flesh, and died on the Cross. This is the measure of His anxiety to make Himself known. He is so eager that we should discover Him that He comes seeking us out. We discover Him, chiefly because He has first discovered us. Probably we would never seek Him at all, unless He had already found us. Our discovery of Him is really the outcome of His prior self-disclosure. If you think of all the people who, in point of fact, have discovered Him, it is clear that anyone can find Him. What a mixed assortment of people were the early discoverers of Jesus! They consisted of quislings like Matthew and national fanatics like Simon the Zealot, of rationalists like Nicodemus and home-spun fishermen like Peter, of prostitutes like the Magdalene and mystics like Mary mother of our Lord, of high and low, rich and poor, old and young, men and women alike. The last person on earth to discover Christ was a brigand whose hand was against every man's, and the first to be welcomed into glory by the same Christ was the saintly Stephen whose face shone like an angel's. Clearly the discovery of Him is open and accessible to all.

Why is it that we are so slow to make this discovery for ourselves? We honour discoverers in other realms. We ourselves rejoice to make new discoveries, to discover new interests, new books, new lands, new hobbies, new ideas, new friends. Why do we hold back from this, the greatest of all discoveries? Why are we so reluctant to explore this world invisible, intangible, which Jesus has so gloriously pioneered? Why are we strangers yet to this Friend of friends, this love divine all human loves excelling? Is it that we are traitors to our own true interests? Is it that, by a kind of fatal perversity, we are prepared to wrong our own souls? Or is it simply that we are ignorant of Christ's value and significance for us? It is said that in the days of the French Revolution the maddened crowd rushed through the corridors of the Tuilleries, bent on the murder of the queen. A young girl was in front of the wild mob, and when they reached the locked door of the royal apartment, she was driven against it with the force of the surging humanity behind her. The door gave way and she was flung bleeding and unconscious on the floor. When the girl came to herself, the beautiful Marie Antoinette was bending over her, gently staunching her bleeding wounds with her own handkerchief. The girl's eyes filled with tears and, bursting into a fit of weeping, she cried, "I never knew till now that you were so beautiful." If we discover Jesus for ourselves, see Him as He is, bending over us with eyes that are the home of all our heart's desirings, we too shall fall in love with Him, and say softly to ourselves, "I never knew till now that you were so beautiful, so precious, so life-transforming, so altogether desirable as this."

V

SOME ARRESTING QUESTIONS

1. THE PLACE OF THE HEART IN RELIGION
(*For Post-Communion*)

"Lovest Thou Me?" (John xxi. 15).

"LOVEST thou me?" This is the question Jesus puts anxiously and intimately to all His disciples. The measure of His anxiety is shown in His thrice-repeated question. It is the only test of discipleship He applied. He might reasonably have asked other questions such as, "Believest thou me?", "Understandest thou me?", "Obeyest thou Me?", "Followest Thou me?" He only asked one question, "Lovest thou Me?" Yet it was enough. In making this solitary demand He was really asking everything. For it is a fundamental and all-inclusive question. On it hang all the Law, the Prophets and the gospel. To meet this claim aright is to satisfy every other. For love is the defence of true morality, the guarantee of right belief, and the spring of all disinterested and effective service. It is therefore of primary importance that we return a right answer to this question. If we have any doubt about our love to Christ, there are a few homely yet searching tests that can be applied, and, as we apply them, let us ask ourselves where we stand in relation to them.

First of all, if we love Jesus, He *will hold the focus of our interest*. Where true love exists, interest in the loved object becomes absorbing and even obsessive. Robert Herrick has a well-known poem called "To Anthea," in which he sings of a passion so commanding that self is obliterated, and lost in its object.

126

> Thou art my life, my love, my heart
> The very eyes of me:
> And hast command of every part,
> To live and die for thee.

All who care to examine the state of their own heart, where love is pure and active, will discover that they only truly live in those they love. A child once defined love as the perfect tense of the verb "to live," which may be bad grammar but is genuine truth. For the whole wealth of our being goes out to those we love. We linger over their physical features, dwell lovingly on their traits of character, take an innocent delight even in their oddities and pecularities. We rejoice in their successes, boast shamelessly of their achievements, drink in avidly words of commendation in their favour which fall from the lips of strangers. We tremble for their weaknesses, weep over their failures, and suffer in their sufferings. Everything that concerns them concerns us. One of Napoleon's officers was badly wounded and needed an operation on his chest. As the surgeon probed deeply, the officer was heard to murmur, "Another inch, and you will find the Emperor." In our love for Jesus, how do we stand up to this test? Does "His image ever fill our hearts and charm our ravished souls"? Are we sufficiently interested in Him to study the records of His earthly life? Do we absorb His words, mark His deeds, suffer in His sufferings, study the grain of His mind and strain of His spirit? Do we trouble to know what others have said and written about Him, His great commentators and expositors, especially Paul and the Apostles? Do we wonderingly dwell on the "Gesta Christi," His contribution to civilised life, since the day He was "received up"? Do we study His contemporary influence? His work of grace in our own hearts, what He has done and is doing for our friends and countless others known to us? Are we thrilled at His growing and greatening influence in the world? Are we deeply pained at the wide-spread indifference to Him and His Gospel in our own land, and at the refusal of earth's mighty ones to make His will supreme in the councils of nations? For be very sure of this, that the measure of our love to Christ is determined by the degree of our interest in Him.

Again, if we love Christ, we shall give *Him the vigour of our minds*. The first commandment, said Jesus, was to love God with all our powers, including our intellect. Jesus is not only the Way and the Life but also the Truth. His religion is not merely a standard of morality, and a scheme of redemption, but also a system of thought. We only honour Jesus aright as we apply our brains to the interpretation and application of His Gospel. "Love," said Pascal, "is a precipitancy of thought. It is thought with morality added to it." The modern disparagement of theology in the interest of practical preaching has no support in the New Testament. The Holy Spirit puts no premium on intellectual sloth. Our Lord's characteristic word to us is, "What think ye?" He offers us His Spirit of truth, but His aid is only available, as we co-operate. Paul tells us that every man should be persuaded in his own mind. He also exhorts us to give reasons for the faith that is in us. And in his Epistles he offers us meat for the full-grown, not milk for babes. Even Peter to whom this question was addressed learned its lesson so well, that to use his own words he "girt up the loins of his mind," and left behind him an Epistle which for sheer beauty and richness is an endless stimulus to all lovers of Christian truth. I am fully aware that intellect is not enough, that indeed pride of intellect may be a denial of Christian love, but to-day the danger is all the other way. What we have to guard against is a sloppy sentimentalism which drains away the mental vitality necessary to a vigorous Christian life and witness. Those who refuse to address themselves to the problems which the Christian faith raises find themselves the prey to every modern heresy, such as Christian Science, Seventh Day Adventism, British Israelitism, and the absurdities of the Milennial Dawnists. One of the implications of loving Christ is to love Him with the mind.

Here is another test. If we love Christ, we shall be eager *to share in His plans and purposes*. We shall want to help forward as much as we can His work in the world. Love's nature is revealed in helpfulness, and its strength tried in sacrifice. We prove our love by our willingness to put at the disposal of others our time, thought, prayers, gifts and sacrifices. A man shows his love to his wife, not so much by what he says to her as by what he is prepared to do for her. It is seen in his willingness to build a home, to share a life, to fulfil a life-purpose. It contains more of the gold of sacrifice than the honey of verbal adulation, of costing-ness than of cosseting. Recently I came across a poem written by the wife of Crabbe, the poet, which deeply moved me. Crabbe was a consumptive and poor, and their lot together was hard. Yet she and her husband loved each other dearly, and before she died, she wrapped her wedding ring in a piece of paper, and on the paper she wrote these lines which her son afterwards read with blinding tears,

> This ring so worn, as you behold,
> So thin, so pale, is yet of gold
> The passion such it was to prove,
> Worn with life's cares, love yet was love.

What a fine thing to have written, and what a testimony! The young girl in the first flush of romance cries, "love is all." The young girl, now a faded woman, worn with years of costly sacrifice, seals with her life-blood her witness to the truth that "love yet is all."

Is this the kind of love we offer to Jesus? Do we prove our love to Him by what we are prepared to do and suffer for Him? Our Lord attached very slight importance to a love for Himself which paid itself with words or exhausted itself in vapid sentiment. An hysterical woman in the crowd once forgot herself so far as to cry, "Blessed is the womb that bare Thee, and the breasts Thou didst suck," only to be greeted with the chilling rejoinder, "Yea rather, blessed are they who hear the word of God and keep it." It is not words Jesus asks of us but works, not profession but practice, not feelings but fulfilment. "If ye love me," said Jesus to His disciples, "keep my commandments." Well, take three of these as tests of leal-hearted love. "Love your enemies, do good to them that hate you, pray for them that despitefully use you." Are we eager to go thus far with Christ in His love adventure? Are we prepared to extend our magnaminity thus far, and launch a love offensive against those hostile frontiers? Or take this command, "Go thou, and do likewise." Jesus is answering the lawyer's question as to who our neighbour is, by telling the immortal story of the "Good Samaritan." Are we prepared, like him, to prove our neighbourly spirit by rendering a service which eats into our time, interrupts our plans, demands the exercise of an active and intelligent sympathy, and costs money? Or take this last command. "Go ye into all the world and preach the Gospel to every creature." How much interest, prayer, intelligence, personal sacrifice are we contributing to the fulfilment of Christ's last and greatest Commission? Our love to Christ is tested and proved by our obedience to His will. He is the Champion of a great Cause, what are we doing to vindicate it? He is the Pioneer of a new Order, what are we doing to establish it on the earth? He is the Sponsor of a divine programme, what are we doing to carry it out? A young man once stood in one of the great art galleries of Europe, studying the picture of the thorn-crowned Christ. He gazed at it long and thoughtfully, and as he turned away was heard softly to murmur, "O Man of Galilee, if you need a helping hand in the stiff battle you are fighting, then count on me." Write your name down as one on whom Christ can count in His great task of world-redemption, and you will prove your love by your deeds.

And here is a final test. If we love Christ, we *shall covet His society as the richest prize of life*. Intimacy with our Lord will be the end of our heart's desire. On human levels this truth is transparently clear. Mutuality of life is the crown of married love. "For this cause shall a man leave father and mother, and cleave unto his wife, and they twain shall be one flesh." The most beautiful illustration of this heart's longing for its affinity is the immortal idyll of Ruth and Naomi. At the parting of the ways "Orpah lifted up her voice and wept," but she honoured her love with nothing but tears. But Ruth clave to Naomi, saying, "Entreat me not to leave thee, nor return from following after thee. For where thou goest I will go, and where thou lodgest I will lodge." She proved her love by coveting the society of Naomi, in scorn of consequence. On kinglier levels such passion of attachment to the Person of Christ is one of the authentic tests of our love to Him. The Magdalene stood without at the sepulchre weeping bitter tears, because the dead form of her Lord meant more to her than all other living earthly interests. The early disciples left home, kindred and career "that they might be with Him." Paul abandoned the brilliant prospects of his Rabbinic career, that he might enjoy Christ's Presence, share in His fortunes, sufferings and triumphs. And are we without a witness of our own? Is He to none of us "the sweetness most ineffable, in whom all joys are found"? If we love Him, we shall seek the secret place where we may commune with Him, heart to heart, spirit with spirit. Rev. Elvit Lewis tells a pretty story about his little boy, who came knocking at his study door, interrupting his studies. He put his hand in his pocket, searching for a piece of chocolate to give him, but the little lad waved it aside, murmuring engagingly, "No daddy, I don't want sweets, I just want to be with you." The whole psychology of private prayer is expressed in that sweet and innocent wish. And not only will we seek the private chamber as a place of intimacy, but we will welcome the privilege of public worship, where we may meet Christ and His friends, to add our quota of adoration and public witness to His grace and glory. So good and pleasant will be the experience, that we shall allow no adverse weather conditions, nor social calls, nor the lure of the highway and the green fields to come between us and the enjoyment of this privilege. Again the Lord's Day will cease to be a problem, for we will honour it in the observance and not in the breach. Once again the Lord's Supper, Christ's trysting place with His people, will be a holy time where we hold high festival in our souls. We shall anticipate it with something of the expectancy and longing with which a lover looks forward to meeting his beloved at the agreed trysting place. If we love Jesus, even death will change its grim visage, for it will be to us merely the last screen, whose rending will disclose to us the Beatific vision. "As Christ means life to me, so death means gain."

These then are some of the tests by which we may discover whether or no we dwell in the love of Christ. As we apply them to our own condition, we may perhaps be feeling how far short we come, and the revelation may be depressing and even disconcerting. We do not love Him with our whole heart and mind and strength. Indeed we may feel like Peter, that we have so often forgotten, denied and even betrayed Him, that the doubt may arise in our mind whether we belong to Him at all. Yet, if we examine our hearts, we shall find, spite of all appearances to the contrary, that somewhere deep in the core of us dwells the vital spark of genuine love to Christ. "Lord, Thou knowest all things, Thou knowest that I love Thee." It is not much more than a spark perhaps, but under the influence of Christ these dying embers may be kindled into a red flaming passion. For Christ has the power to do this, if we give what we have. The final guarantee that this may be so is not our love to Him, but His love to us. We never need to ask Him the wistful question He puts to us, "lovest Thou me." His love is demonstrated to us by what He has done and suffered for us. On the Cross His love, as Browning wrote, "burst and blossomed into a rage to suffer for mankind." Let us not then dwell so much on our hold on Him, as on His mighty grasp of us. Someone wrote of Goethe, "Other men I love with my own strength, he teaches me to love with his strength." "We love Him, because He first loved us," and He teaches us to continue to love Him, not with our strength but His. In the words of Christina Rosetti,

Because Thy love hath sought me
  All mine is thine, and thine is mine,
Because Thy love hath bought me
  I will not be mine own but thine.

I lift my heart to Thy heart
  Thy heart, sole resting-place for mine.
Shall Thy heart crave for my heart
  And shall not mine crave back for Thine?

2. THE CURE FOR SPIRITUAL INVALIDISM
(*For Lent*)

Wilt thou be made whole? (John v. 6).

This incident is meant by the writer of this Gospel to be spiritualised. It is one of a group of seven miracles, each of which is designed to reveal some aspect of our Lord's office for men. Here we see Him represented as the Healer of the worst type of spiritual disease. Bethesda, which means the house of mercy, may fittingly symbolise the Christian Church, and the pool that surrounded it as "the fountain opened for sin and uncleanness." Around its porches are gathered to-day, as then "a great multitude of impotent folk, blind, halt and withered, waiting for the moving of the waters" of the Spirit to help them in their distress. Perhaps they have waited so long for something to happen, and been so frequently disappointed that now the hope of any cure has faded out. Hence the relevance of this question, "Wilt thou be made whole?" or in Moffatt's rendering, "Do you want your health restored?"

To begin with, we must emphasise the fact that this *is a serious question*. On the surface we might think otherwise. We can almost hear the instinctive protest coming from this puzzled patient, "Why should I be where I am, if I did not want to be cured? Why should I endure the discomfort and fatigue of these long weary years of waiting, if my purpose was not serious? Surely this exhausting experience of mine is its own evidence of my resolute will for health." One or two considerations, however, give us room for pause. Was this man after all as powerless to help himself as he claimed to be? He was not incapable of movement, as he tells us himself, only of moving swiftly enough. His trouble was, "that always someone else gets in before me." What was to hinder him from dragging himself to the edge of the pool, of sitting in it, if need be? Can we really accept this statement, that no one was prepared to give him a helping hand in his extremity? The suspicion begins to grow on us that his will for health was not as pronounced as he would have us believe.

This question exposes much of the spiritual impotence to be found in all our churches. How comes it that in so many lives that claim to belong to Christ there are present so few of the fruits of the Spirit? Why this chronic condition of spiritual ill-health? Why all these weaknesses and defilements that still cling to us? Thirty-eight years, it may be, we have pledged our allegiance to Christ, and yet we have little to show in the way of Christian growth and maturity; thirty-eight years of contact with the means of grace, and yet our violent tempers are unsubdued and our tongues uncontrolled; thirty-eight years of preaching and teaching, yet we are still uninstructed in the faith, lukewarm in our devotion, halting in our witness, slack in the exercise of our gifts, unconvincing in our impact on the world? Why this lengthy and dismal record of feebleness, impotence and frustration? It is not natural, seemly or right. Such a condition demands an explanation. Streams of divine healing are ceaselessly moving towards us. The medicines and cordials of the Gospel are accessible to all who claim them to heal and invigorate. Why are they failing to produce their proper effect in us? It has become a serious question whether we want to be restored to health.

Again, *this is a revealing question*. It raises the whole issue as to whether or no we really wish to be delivered from the incubus of our frailties, and to recover the normal use of our God-given powers. It is a question we must not answer lightly, for it cuts deep into the sub-soil of motive, habit and desire. "Wilt thou be made whole?" This is one of these unexpected and disconcerting questions which our Lord was in the habit of asking. This man was obviously startled by it. The moment it was put he felt its cutting edge and tried to burke it. He went off at a tangent, tried to "rationalise" his behaviour by laying the blame on circumstances. He refused to face the truth that he had become habituated to his condition, reconciled to it, indeed had come rather to like it. It is quite possible to develop an invalid complex. Invalidism has its capacity to build up its own defence mechanisms, by which it seeks to buttress itself against the shock of reality, and the fatigue of facing the responsibilities of an active life. This particular case of course was pathological, brought about by long years of inactivity. Normally a sick patient is eager and anxious to rid himself of his weakness. He has no desire to be an invalid. He consults the best doctors, spends money lavishly, travels to sunny climes, undergoes a strick regimen of diet, and so forth, to recover health. This eager anxiety for health does not hold good in the spiritual realm. Few people desire to be physical wrecks, but many are quite content to be moral profligates. Sin drags us to itself with chains which we are not at all anxious to break. Sin feeds upon itself, makes its own claims, creates its own appetites and desires. The devils who possessed the Gadarene maniac had only one request to make of Jesus, "Leave us alone." It would be easy to help the helpless if they desired to be helped. This man's problem could at any time be resolved if he were anxious for a solution. What Christ's question reveals is that we could all be very different people from what we are, if we desired this change enough. R. L. Stevenson tells us that the Master of Ballantrae was leaving Durisdeer, and he said to MacKellar, his faithful henchman, "Do you think that I have no regrets?" "I don't think," was the answer, "that you could be so bad a man, if you had not all the machinery for being a good man." "No," said the other wistfully, "No, not all the machinery. Not all. You are there in error. The malady of not wanting, my cunning evangelist."

Once again this is *an indispensable question*. It is a prior question which must be asked of us and answered by us before any curative process can set in. The reason is that sustained and rightly directed desire is the only effective agent in spiritual change. For it is not acuteness of insight, nor right judgment, nor persuasive argument, nor even moral consent that lifts us out of the morass of spiritual impotence so much as passionate and dominant desire. "Blessed are they that hunger and thirst after righteousness, for they shall be filled." It is generally conceded that the chief factor in spiritual change is the will, but the strength of the will does not lie in the pressure we put upon it, but in the strength of the motives that play upon it. It is our dominant desire that fixes the strength and shapes the direction of the will, and it is the altered will that changes character. No physician can cure a patient who is set on remaining an invalid. No teacher can impart instruction to a pupil who refuses to learn. No saviour can find the lost, if they wilfully elude his search. Every problem of human regeneration is in the last resort a matter of one's dominant desires. In the book of Acts an incident occurs relating to a certain man at Lystra who had never walked. Paul, fixing his gaze on him, perceived that "he had faith to be made whole." So Paul said to him, "Stand upon thy feet." Up he jumped and began to walk. Here was a man controlled by the desire to be made whole, so he was ready for any possibilities that might emerge. As for this other man under discussion, here our Lord gravely doubted both the genuineness and intensity of his desire for health. Hence the relevance of this question and its necessity.

Do you desire to have your health restored? That is the searching and necessary question Christ puts to each of us now. Do you want to be different from what you are? Would you take health at Christ's hands as a gift? Do you want to live a life of temperance and moderation, to have purity of heart and spiritual soundness, to enjoy communion with God through Christ, to live on His exalted level of life? Or if such desire be lacking, do you desire to have the desire? Then Christ will take you even on that level, and bring into active exercise desires that do not yet exist. He has the capacity to stir desire within our torpid souls, send up warm currents to the will, and release the frozen immobility of our inner being. This man made two discoveries on that memorable day when Jesus visited Bethesda, one that desire within him was wan and wasted, and the other that he now desperately wanted to be healed. If this is our state, then we have reached the point where we are prepared to accept Christ's prescription for curing spiritual invalidism. This can be stated quite simply and briefly. There are really three separate stages in a complete cure, and all who seek spiritual health should follow and practise each one separately.

To the impotent man, startled, expectant, and now alive to the possibility of a cure, Jesus says, "*Rise.*" In other words, He exhorts him to do the thing which for thirty-eight years he was powerless to do. Encouraged by Christ he made the requisite effort, and to his amazement he found himself standing on his feet. Here we run into the central miracle of the Christian faith, a miracle which may be repeated here and now. The miracle is that the living Christ, by the power of His spirit can work effects in a man's personality which no effort of his will, nor any process of auto-suggestion can achieve. Christ's chief work is always wrought out in the realm of the impossible. To the man with the withered hand He said, "Stretch out thy hand" and in obedience to Christ he did it. To Lazarus in the tomb, a sheeted corpse, dead and rotting, He cries, "Lazarus, Come forth!" and in obedience to Christ he came forth. To the paralysed man He said, "Rise!" and he rose. Christ's commands are always promises, and His promises are always powers. The eternal miracle of the Gospel is, that Jesus Christ gives to men, to any man who believes in and trusts Him, the power to be and do what in his own strength he could neither be nor do. Christ Jesus says, "Rise!"

Carrying the process of cure still further, Jesus next commands the man to *take up his* bed, or more accurately, "Lift your mat!" In other words, "Remove the symbol of your infirmity." Strike away the prop which confirms you in your invalidism. Make no provision for a relapse. Learn to sink or swim. Pitch away that handy mat which bolsters up your invalid-complex. Fling ruthlessly aside every support on which formerly you leaned, every object which inflames your vices, every artificial stimulant which confirms you in your weakness. "Make no provision for the flesh, to fulfil the lusts thereof." In that Stevensonian study of dual personality, *Dr. Jekyll and Mr. Hyde*, Dr. Jekyll became ashamed of his depraved alter-ego, Mr. Hyde. He resolved to cease to play the rôle of the anti-social scoundrel Hyde, but his purpose failed because of one fatal error in tactics. He forgot to roll up his mat. He still kept beside him the secret vials and chemicals by means of which he effected his transference of personalities. Nay worse, he kept in a secret cupboard *the clothes of Mr. Hyde*. He was merely asking for trouble. The Devil came back like a roaring lion. It is not only sound Christianity but good psychology to remove all traces of our former weakness, to burn our bridges behind us, to eliminate all incentives to a relapse, and to create such a situation for ourselves that, if we fail, we have nothing to fall back upon but the strong arms of the living Christ.

Finally, Christ issued the command, "WALK!" That is, to exercise consciously and continuously the new powers that you have acquired. Get out of the entire area of your former weakness, and multiply your contacts and interests in the new sphere to which you have committed yourself. "Walk!" Launch yourself boldly into the new adventure of health, casting no sickly lingering look behind you. Not only make no provision for the flesh, but put on the Lord Christ. The best defence against falling into sin is to be passionately devoted to goodness. The best way to guard against relapse into the old life is to be a vigorous adventurer in the new. If you have been an alcoholic addict become a Temperance reformer, a gambler, join an anti-gambling league, a victim of impurity, help to further a purity campaign. Exercise yourself in all godliness. Practise habits of spiritual discipline. Study the Bible. Seek the secret place of prayer. Diligently use the means of grace. Associate with Christian people. Engage in Christian enterprises. Give all diligence to make your calling and election sure. "Walk!"

It is worth noticing that the next time we see this man he is in the Temple. There he learns who Jesus is, receives further instructions and warnings from Him, and is set more firmly on the way to "walk." Nature, we are told, abhors a vacuum, so does the regenerated life. The empty life is the unguarded life. The life filled with Christian interests and activities is the only saved and safe life. "This I say unto you, *walk* in the Spirit and you shall not fulfil the lusts of the flesh."

It was the Sabbath day when this man was made whole. May we not hope that some such miracle may now take place, as Jesus once again visits His church, and uses the means of grace to set the spiritually paralysed upon their feet! Such miracles of grace are still being endlessly repeated, and it remains for each one of us to receive the gifts He offers, and carry with us on our way some witness of our own to the Saviour's healing virtue.

3. The Problem of Lives Cut Short
(*For Armistice Sunday*)

Are there not twelve hours in the day? (John xi. 9).

Multitudes of people to-day are perplexed with the problem of unfinished lives. It has been forced on their attention by the tragic wars of our time. The casualty lists of war, consisting as they do of young men in their twenties, give even the most unreflective furiously to think.

This is, of course, not specifically a wartime problem. In days of comparative security and quiet, young men, women and even children, die long before their allotted span. Disease, accident, natural calamity as well as war, claim their victims among the very young as well as the aged. Yet no one will deny that wartime conditions acutely sharpen the issue, and make the burden of its solution more oppressive. In normal times the death of the young, tragic though it be, is frequent enough, but the experience after all is exceptional. In these days, however, the balance is tilted all the other way, and death reaps too rich a harvest in the unlikely field of youth. This whole question raises vexed and profoundly disturbing thoughts about the nature of the Providential order. To speak in any cheap or facile way on an issue so deep, on which men feel so keenly, would be an impertinence. There are, however, certain suggestions worth considering which may be of some help to sorely puzzled and burdened hearts.

To begin with, it is a comfort to remember *the place of Providence in the number of our hours*. According to Jesus the end as well as the beginning of our earthly life is decreed by God. In the eleventh chapter of John's Gospel we have the locus classicus on this question. It arose out of the announcement of our Lord to His disciples of His intention to return to Judaea. The disciples remonstrated, "Master, the Jews of late sought to stone Thee, and goest Thou thither again?" Jesus answered, "Are there not twelve hours in the day?" The implications of this position are that the measure of His days would be determined, not by His enemies, but by God. He would depart this life, not at the stroke of accident or disease, nor by the deadly thrust of malignant foes, but at the summons of His Father's will. Till the curfew of God rang to call Him home He would abide in His lot and continue to fulfil His mission, and no power on earth could lengthen or shorten the number of His hours.

This conception of a divinely fixed limit to a man's tenure of life was a leading idea in the mind of Jesus. It was the burden of His message to "that fox Herod." "Behold," He said, "I cast out devils, and I do cures to-day and to-morrow, and the third day I shall be perfected." . . . To Pilate who claimed the power of life and death over Him He said, "Thou couldst have no power at all against me except it were given thee from above." If we could only accept Christ's view of Providence and rest in it, it would mitigate the asperity of our lot, and reconcile us to its changes and shocks. It would conserve for us all the values of endurance and resignation that are usually associated with the pagan doctrine of Fatalism. It would help to fortify our troubled hearts with the reflection that the end of life is decreed, not by blind chance, or purposeless Fate, but by an intelligent and purposeful will. It would also give us the knowledge that no life lived in God, whose end is fixed by God, can be incomplete or cut off before its appointed time. Every man is immortal till his work is done. If we believe, as we readily do, that our *ways* are ordered of God, why should we hesitate to accept the position that our *days* are also fixed in the calendar of Heaven? And if this be so, then it is part of our faith to commit, without fret or care, the number of our hours to God's keeping, and to learn to say with the poet—

> Lord, it belongs not to my care
> Whether I die or live;
> To love and serve Thee is my share
> And this Thy grace must give.

A further degree of comfort can be gathered from the reflection that *the true measurement of life is not in length of days*. "Years are not life. Years are but the shells of life, and empty shells, if they hold only days and days and days." Mere prolongation of existence on the earthly plane is not in itself a necessary nor indeed always a desirable boon. Jesus suggests in this very connection that extension of life beyond the divine appointment may be an unmitigated curse. To claim thirteen days when God offers us twelve, to seek to secure them by sullying our honour, or playing the coward, or declining the risks of life is in the end a spiritually disastrous course. "If a man walk in the night, he stumbleth because there is no light in him." *Length of days* is not what we should ask from life, but *quality of living*. It is intensity, richness, fullness of being, that give significance to the passing days. And if we extract this divine essence from life, can we justly complain that even the briefest day is too short? Viewed under this light the problem of the incomplete life takes on another and different aspect. Who are we that we can claim the right to say that even a brief life has not been fully lived? If "ripeness is all" as Shakespeare contended, may not the experiences which war brings enormously hasten the process of maturity? Eternity may be packed into an hour. In a short time a man may fulfil a long time. One crowded hour of glorious life may be worth an age without a name. Is it not possible that the added quality given to a shortened day may more than compensate for the brevity of its duration? We cannot and may not forget that it was a young man who was crucified on Calvary. He died with the dew of youth fresh on His brow. Yet in His inner consciousness there is no hint that He had been unjustly treated or had died too soon. On the contrary there is every reason to believe that He was perfectly satisfied with things as they were and that he had lived a full and complete life. "I have finished the work Thou hast given me to do." "Ripeness is all."

Further it will help us in considering this vexed question to reflect that *there are not less than twelve hours in every day.* Generally when considering the matter of Time what we stress is the truth that there are not more than twelve hours in the day. And to be sure this is a sound and sobering reflection. In the Jewish Talmud occur these words, "Life is a shadow, but is it the shadow of a tree that stands? Nay, rather it is the shadow of a bird on the wing. Away flieth the bird, and neither bird nor shadow leave a vestige behind." That aspect of truth was also present to the mind of our Lord and in other connections He draws earnest attention to it. "I must work the works of Him Who sent me, while it is day, for the night cometh when no man can work." He ordered His own life and asks us to order ours to the beat and speed of Time's hurrying feet. But here in the passage before us what holds His mind is not the *brevity* of life but its *sufficiency*. If it is a solemnising thought that there are *not more* than twelve hours, it is equally a comforting and tonic reflection that there are *not less* than twelve hours in the day.

Twelve hours in the day are not many. Even as we count them they are ringing to evensong already. There is no time to waste, but there is time enough to do what God demands. In the case of our Lord His brief life sufficed to finish the work God gave Him to do. He had ample time to exhibit to the world the beauty of a stainless character, to preach the Gospel of the Kingdom of God, and to set loose those spiritual forces which are redeeming the world. Each man's life, be it long or short as reckoned by figures on a dial, is yet long enough to reveal his worth, to make his contribution, to realise his destiny, to do the will of God. Even the life of an infant has a mission to fulfil, ere it swiftly passes to behold the face of its angels in Heaven. And these young victims of war who fall on the field of honour, have they failed to realise the purpose for which their lives were given? Nay, say rather that dying in their prime they have bequeathed richer gifts than gold—the memory of heroic deeds, the inspiration of costly sacrifice, the positive achievement of conserving for the benefit of mankind the higher values of life. "Never was so much owed by so many to so few," was the tribute paid by a Premier to our Air Force. Had they lived to the age of Methuselah, could they have done more for the human race, or indeed as much? And if the purchase price of these boons is an early death, will anyone say that their lives are incomplete?

> The period of our life is brief,
> It is the red in the red rose leaf,
> It is the gold of the summer sky,
> It is the flight of the bird on high.

> But we may fill the space
> With such infinite grace
> That the red shall vein all time,
> And the gold through all ages shine,
> And the bird fly swift and straight
> To the portals of Heaven's gate.

There remains yet another plea to be advanced to ease the pressure of our tragic human situation, namely this, that in the final reckoning *there are more days than one*. Here on earth there are twelve hours in the day, but in the hereafter there is another day where the hours are not counted, because Time is no more. If you press for reasons for holding to this heartening assurance, much could be said in its defence from the side of Revelation, reason and instinct. For the moment let this suffice, that the manifest incompleteness of life even at its longest stretch demands a future sphere of reference for its fulfilment. At its shortest stretch the argument is even more cogent and compelling. There is really no final solution of the problem of the unfinished life till it is set down in the context of eternity. If this life be all, then we must conclude that it is a broken column and meaningless. "Truly," Browning makes Paracelsus say—

> Truly there needs another life to come:
> If this be all . . .
> And other life awaits us not—for one
> I say 'tis a poor cheat, a stupid bungle,
> A wretched failure. I, for one protest
> Against it, and I hurl it back with scorn.

Another day with its uncounted hours is the only view of the matter that makes sense. To think otherwise is to make our life planless and its Architect resourceless and heartless. It is to charge the Father of our spirits with giving His children a promise it is beyond His power to keep. We must hold firmly to the position that there is another life where "all instincts immature," "all purposes unsure," come to glorious fruition. "In Eden every flower is blown," and Heaven doth make perfect this imperfect life. Let us then gather to our tortured hearts the comfort of these assurances and believe, as we have every right to believe, that those young lives that have passed so swiftly from our earthly vision have not been short-circuited nor plunged into eternal darkness, but connect on a higher plane of light and life and love, and shine as the stars for ever and ever.

A friend of mine, the late Mr. D. D. Binnie, a lawyer in Glasgow, lost a son of his in the last war. To relieve his grief and also to comfort those in a like case, he wrote the following poem. It was originally published in *The Thistle* Souvenir Book, the proprietors of which I hope will pardon its use here.

To Any Parent

Say not the boy is dead, but rather say
He's but a little further on the way,
Impatient sooner to behold the view—
At the next turning you may see it too.
Say he's a child again, early to bed,
On night's soft pillow fain to lay his head.
Say he is off to track the mountain stream
And lingers by the side in boyish dream.
Say by immortal waters now at rest
He clasps a thousand memories to his breast.
Say to his wondering quests wise angels smiling
Tell the true story of the world's beguiling.
Say on heroic task his soul is thrilling
Where noble dream hath noble deed's fulfilling.
Say to high festival he moves in state
Enfranchised, aureoled, immaculate.
Say that he feasts with comrades tried and true,
But in his heart the banquet waits for you.
Say, in the Presence, at a gentle word
He shows the wound-marks to his wounded Lord.
Say never he is dead, but rather say
He's but a little further on the way.

4. THE CHALLENGE OF THE CROSS
(*For Good Friday*)

Are ye able to drink the cup that I am about to drink? (Matt. xx. 22).

Did these sons of Zebedee really know what they promised, when they asserted their ability to drink Christ's cup? Did they know that the baptism with which He was about to be baptised was the baptism of the Cross? Did they realise the implications of the obligation they had so lightly accepted? Were they prepared to accept the grim challenge of the Cross? The Cross may be approached from many angles. It may be regarded as an historical event, as a deed in time, as something that happened at Jerusalem in the reign of Pontius Pilate. Or it may be regarded as a gospel, as an act of God by which sinners estranged from Him were reconciled to Him. Or it may be regarded as a theology, by which it is possible to state in words its significance for thought. But there is still a fourth way of assessing its significance, and that is to look on it in the light of a spiritual discipline, a culture of the soul, a way of living, in other words to regard it in the light of challenge. Now, if we accept the challenge of the Cross, to what kind of life does it commit us? What kind of people should we be and what manner of life should we practise, if we follow the way of the holy and venerable Cross?

First of all it commits us to the *exercise of a spirit of undiscourageable good-will*. If the Cross means anything in terms of human behaviour, it means precisely that. It exhibits a limitless magnanimity expressed in circumstances of crucial difficulty. When Jesus came to earth, the angels heralded His birth as the dawn of a new era of "good-will to men." By explicit exhortation and in parable after parable He taught that doctrine. On the Cross He practised what He preached, and refused all the overtures of His enemies to retaliate in kind. He kept on loving the men who would fain have dragged Him down to their level, and with His dying breath He breathed a prayer to God for the forgiveness of His murderers.

> Thy foes might hate, despise, revile,
> Thy friends unfaithful prove;
> Unwearied in forgiveness still,
> Thy heart could only love.

Here we have a new ethic, a new code of behaviour, a new reaction to sin. It is quite startlingly new and revolutionary. The like of it was never seen nor practised before. Magnanimity was not unknown in pagan circles. There were isolated instances here and there, but they were quite exceptional, and generally created surprise. The normal code, practised and commended everywhere, was what Xenophon wrote about Cyrus the younger, "No one did more good to his friends, or more mischief to his enemies." Judaism mercifully limited the law of revenge to retaliation in kind. "An eye for an eye, and a tooth for a tooth," that, and no more. But Jesus' demand was for an all-out offensive of good-will. "Love your enemies, do good to them that hate you, etc." When the blinded Samson was taken to the Temple to make sport for the Philistines, he seized the pillars and prayed to God for strength to tear down the Temple that he might be avenged of his enemies. The soldiers made sport of Jesus round the Cross, and the priests jeered at Him, but Jesus retaliated by praying, "Father, forgive them, for they know not what they do." That was a technique that was new, sensational and also creative. It was His solution of the problem of evil. It was His tactics for breaking the entail of sin. It was His technique for leading sin's captivity captive. This is not passive but active resistance. It is an all-out offensive of good-will, an endeavour to turn the flank of the enemy by meeting cruelty with kindness, insult with forbearance, injustice with magnanimity, and hatred with love.

This is one challenge at least which the Cross presents to us to-day. No one need lack an opportunity for accepting that challenge. The field for its exercise is as wide as the world. Everywhere we look we see evidences of suspicion, bitterness and hate. The world seems to be inoculated with prussic acid rather than with the spirit of Christ. Class war, colour strife, ideological tensions, racial animosities, national antagonisms abound. Communism as a matter of policy stirs up class strife and preaches a gospel of hate. And even within the Christian Church exist cleavages, divisions and antipathies.

Perhaps, however, it is in our own personal relations with others that we feel the cutting edge of this challenge most acutely. What is our normal reaction to injustices done to ourselves? How do we think of, and behave to, those who deal treacherously with us, who work against us, who overreach us, misrepresent us, besmirch our character, lower our prestige and wound our pride? The old Adam in us dies hard. There is a deep core of self in all of us which deeply resents any slight, fancied or real, done to us. This raw nerve of self, when touched by an unfriendly hand, quivers and writhes with spite and rancour. The inclination to hit back, to get even with the offender, to compensate for wrong done by retaliation in kind, is almost overwhelming. The biographer of Stalin writes, "Stalin never forgot nor forgave an injury done to him. He bided his time and in the end always hit back." Compare with this the saying of Luther, "My soul is too glad and too great to be at heart the enemy of any man." The Christian's revenge is to accept the challenge of the Cross. It is to counter hate and retaliation with an un-discourageable spirit of good-will. Listen to the words of a great Christian Jew who had at one time been a specialist in hate. "As God's own chosen then, as consecrated and beloved, be clothed with compassion, kindness, humility, gentleness and good-temper—forbear and forgive each other in any case of complaint; As Christ forgave you, so must you forgive. And above all you must be loving, for love is the link of the perfect life" (Moffatt). Paul had accepted this part of the challenge of the Cross.

A second challenge the Cross presents is the *necessity of self-identification with the sins and sufferings of humanity.*

This was the hall-mark of all Christ's earthly life. Even the common people noticed it. They remarked on His resemblance to Jeremiah, whose heart, as they remembered, was stricken for the hurt of his people. On the Cross the full weight of our human burden was laid on His shoulders. There can be little doubt that the main element in His sufferings was their vicarious nature. He was stricken for the transgressions of His people. The Lord God laid on Him the inquity of us all. The bearing of that burden of sin, and its consequences in human suffering, is what the Cross means. Jowett speaks of Him there as "a divine seismograph," delicately registering in his sensitive heart the faintest tremors of the world's sin and woe: "desperate tides of the world's great anguish forced through the channels of a single heart." If that is what the Cross meant to Jesus, then its perpetual challenge for us is that we should reproduce in our lives something of the same divine compassion and sympathy.

Paul in one passage in Colossians speaks of the Christian vocation as "filling up that which is lacking in the sufferings of Christ," as if in Christ's Passion there was something left which only we could implement. And in Philippians he declares it to be his ambition to know Christ and "the fellowship of His sufferings." One would suppose that Paul was sufficiently initiated into these sufferings already. He, least of all, should reproach himself in this regard. For, as he tells his Corinthian converts, his Christian life was a daily crucifixion. Yet no: spite of labours more abundant, of his sufferings and perils and cares for the gospel, he had not yet fully accepted the challenge of the Cross. He had not yet fully drained the cup Christ put to His lips. This was a prayer he offered, a plea, the expression of an ideal, something he had yet to reach, and only by reaching it could he be said to know Christ fully: spite of his great record of service and sacrifice the Cross demanded a richer implication of himself into the needs of suffering humanity.

The challenge of the Cross must mean as much for us too. It must mean the extension of our personalities to the dimensions of an all-inclusive sympathy. Our hearts also must be like seismographs, registering the agitations which disturb human lives. We must be able to say with Walt Whitman, "Agonies are my changes of raiment. I do not ask to be the wounded man. I am the wounded man." Or like Ezekiel in exile we must learn to say, "I sat where they sat." We shall never reach any success in Christian service till we "are baptised into a feeling sense of all conditions." This intense and extended sympathy is a primary requisite for all effective evangelical and missionary work. I spent six months in Calcutta lately, that city of fully four million souls, the headquarters of fanatical Hinduism (the name Calcutta is derived from the Kali Ghat, the notorious shrine of Kali there). I asked myself what it must mean to do Christian work in a heathen city like that, with its squalor, disease, ignorance and abject poverty. To accept the challenge of the Cross in such circumstances must mean suffering. It carries with it the obligation to bear their sins, their pride of caste, their superstition, lust and greed. It must mean bearing their poverty, their disease, their heartache, dull misery and sheer despair. "When Jesus saw the multitudes He was moved with compassion on them, because they fainted, and were scattered abroad, as sheep without a shepherd." Such sympathy is a terrible and costly gift to ask or receive. But it is the price we must pay for effective Christian service. It is what it means to accept the challenge of the Cross. In Christian work there is no healing without feeling, no blessing without bleeding. It remains abidingly true, that it is only "they who sow in tears that shall reap in joy. He that goeth forth and weepeth, bearing precious seed, shall doubtless come again with rejoicing, bringing his sheaves with him."

The third challenge of the Cross *is a clarion call to endurance*. Have you ever sat down, and reflected on the Cross and envisaged to yourself, what in terms of endurance it meant for Christ? There were all the circumstances leading up to the Cross. There were the trials, both ecclesiastical and civil, which in themselves were severe tests of endurance. Then there were the shocking misrepresentations of His motives made before the Roman authorities and the Sanhedrin. They accused Him, the lover of truth, of being a liar. They charged Him, who awesomely reverenced His Father, with being a blasphemer. They alleged that He "stirred up the people" whose one aim was to bring "peace on earth." These charges against His honour must have been hard to endure. And then there was the Roman torture. The flagellum, as it was called was a cruel thing. Many of its victims fainted, or went mad, or even died. On the top of that came the actual crucifying. "He bare our sins in His own body on the tree." On this Dr. Denney observes, "Don't forget that the body was flesh and blood, and the tree was nails and timber." He endured that long drawn out agony, and as if all that were not enough, there had to be added to it what the Scriptures call "the reproach of the Cross." There were the staring vulgar mob, the bespattering of His face with spittle, the wagging heads of the priests who mocked at His weakness, saying, "He saved others, Himself He cannot save." It may be, as we are constantly reminded, that others besides Jesus had to endure the Cross. That is so, but none had to endure "such contradiction of sinners against Himself." And none endured with such kingly dignity, such absence of rancour, such patience and humility, and such victory over Himself.

> No ungentle murmuring word
> Escaped His silent tongue.

When Robertson of Brighton was told that such fearless advocacy of truth was alienating the ecclesiastical authorities, he said, "I don't care." When he was further reminded that he was outraging public sentiment he replied again, "I don't care." "Do you know what happened to 'Don't care'?" they continued. "Yes," he replied sorrowfully, "He was crucified on Calvary." Jesus with a kind of sublime recklessness seemed to disregard the consequences to Himself of the course He was pursuing. At all costs He must finish the work His Father gave Him to do. Sooner than compromise on this main issue, sooner than deny the truth, betray His trust,

deviate by a hairsbreadth from the line of God's appointment, He would endure to the end, without malice,
complaint, or sense of injustice the whole grievous burden
laid upon His shoulders. He would drink to the last and
bitterest dregs the cup the Father gave Him, which our
sins had mingled for Him.

No one can gaze on such a spectacle of iron endurance
without feeling the muscles of his will tightening. No one
can contemplate this Man of sorrows on His Cross, facing
death with quiet indomitable endurance, and then gaze
on his own life, without feeling the pulse of his resolve
quickening. These are the questions the challenge of the
Cross raises in our minds. Have we the power to endure
hardness like good soldiers of Jesus Christ? Can we fight
the good fight of faith and not heed the wounds, toil and
ask for no reward save that of doing God's will? Are we
for a great, good cause able to face unpopularity, hardship,
loneliness, misunderstanding, and above all, indifference?
Can we keep right on to the end of the road, without
giving in, without capitulating, compromising, or com-
plaining, even if we meet opposition and apparent failure?
Can we continue to work without reward, toil without
return, suffer without bitterness, and endure without
retaliation? That is what the challenge of the Cross means
in terms of endurance.

If we find it difficult or impossible to meet his demand
let us take another long look at the Cross of our Lord.
There is a great passage in Hebrews xii which is generally
misinterpreted. The writer has catalogued in the previous
chapter a long list of the heroes of the faith who "endured,
as seeing Him who is invisible." He then proceeds to draw
the lesson. "Therefore as we have so vast a throng of
witnesses surrounding us, let us discard every encum-
brance and besetting sin." Generally that is taken to
mean that the celestial throng is gazing on us strugglers,
and encouraging us, like spectators in an amphitheatre, to
run a steadfast course. But Prof. W. Manson, in his recent
fine book on Hebrews, represents them as gazing, not at
us, but at Jesus in glory. Let us also, like them, gaze on

the same enthroned Jesus, and what is the vision we get then? We see Jesus, "the Pioneer and Consummator of our faith, who, for the joy set before Him, endured the Cross." Dr. Manson suggests an interesting variant. "Who, instead of the joy set before Him, that is, the joy He experienced in His pre-Incarnate life, instead of the felicity He experienced in the bosom of the Father, bravely accepted the Cross, disregarding its shame." And now comes the pith and marrow of the matter for us. "Just reflect what it meant for Him to face so courageously all that opposition of sinful men to Himself—that you may not grow faint and weary in your souls." To keep close to the Cross is the only way to accept its challenge.

The last challenge of the Cross we shall mention is its *call to a life of self-renunciation*. All Christ's earthly life was a life of self-emptying. He was the only man born of woman of whom it can be truly said that He pleased not Himself. His meat was to do the will of His Father, and to finish His work. Yes, but in the finishing of that work He was called upon to endure the Cross, and that was the severest test of His devotion to God's will He had yet faced. How excruciating the ordeal was may be gathered from His bloody sweat in the Garden. That agony represents the violence of the struggle for the suppression of self. And when He reached the point of saying, "Not my will but thine be done," He registered not a meek sub-mission to the inevitable, but a final and successful assault on the ramparts of His self-will. The Cross was merely a placarding in a public and emphatic way of the complete-ness of His self-renunciation. As He marched to His Cross like a Conquerer, He neither asked nor accepted sympathy nor pity. To the women of Jerusalem, beating their breasts in sympathy, He said, "Daughters of Jerusalem, weep not for Me but for yourselves." Everyone knows who has suffered great bodily pain, how all-absorbing and self-demanding it can be. It obliterates almost every other interest. Yet Jesus, suspended on His Cross, tortured and racked with pain long drawn out, refused every palliative, asked for no one's sympathy, showed no signs of wounded pride nor weak self-pity. On the contrary, as He hung there, He was so completely detached from self, so objective in His outlook, that He was free to pray for His murderers, to offer salvation to a penitent malefactor, and to make provision for His mother's future. It was this total absence of self, and complete devotion to God's will that was the saving element in His atoning death.

Here is another great challenge the Cross binds upon us. It calls us to live no longer to ourselves but to Him who loved us and gave Himself for us. Herein lies the major problem of the Christian life. Our vocation as Christians is to suppress and as far as possible to eliminate the self-life. It is the intrusive claims of this graceless, greedy, demanding self that are the main obstacle to effective Christian service. We spoil or at least mar nearly all our usefulness by our morbid craving for recognition, applause or reward. We often forget that our first obligation, as the followers of the selfless Christ, is to do God's will, not our own. Henry Drummond puts the matter plainly. "The end of the Christian life is not to do good, nor to get good, nor even to be good. It is just to do what God wills, whether that be winning or losing, suffering or recovering, living or dying." Jesus Himself leaves us in no doubt as to what discipleship means. "If any man would be my disciple, let Him say 'no' to self, and take up his own cross of self-renunciation, and follow me. For whosoever shall save His life shall lose it." When we have reached the point of saying, "none of self, and all of Thee," we have accepted this challenge of the Cross.

Where then do we stand in relation to the great challenges the Cross of Christ addresses to us to-day? When the Scottish National Covenant was being signed at Greyfriars, Lord Warriston gave utterance to these historic words. "We are come to the parting of the ways. There is the King of England's way and ours. Ours is the way of honour and freedom. It is narrow. It is hard. It is dark and uncertain. But he has neither a Christian nor a Scottish heart who will face this crisis without taking part." Life presents us all with these stark alternative choices.

There is the broad and the narrow way, the low and the high, the way of self-pleasing and the way of self-renunciation. There can be no doubt in any one's mind as to which of these two ways the Cross of Christ calls us. "Are you able to drink this cup of which I am about to drink?" Shall our response not be this?

> O Cross that liftest up my head,
>   I dare not ask to fly from Thee;
> I lay in dust life's glory dead,
> And from the ground there blossoms red
>   Life that shall endless be.

5. Love and Sorrow at the Tomb
(*For Easter*)

Jesus saith unto her, Woman, why weepest thou? (John xx. 15).

This is a lovely vignette, full of human interest, and rich in dramatic touches which grip the heart. Mary of Magdala is alone in the garden, because she cannot bring herself to leave the place where the body of her dear Lord was laid. She stooped over the sepulchre, peered into it, and as she stooped her salt tears dropped into the empty tomb. She is weeping because it is empty, and because, in the bitterness of her heart, she believed it had been rifled. That was to her the only possible explanation of the empty tomb. It never occurred to her in her wildest dreams that the cause of her sorrow was, if rightly understood, an occasion for rapturous joy. But that is another matter. Meantime let us linger beside her at this sacred spot, and see what lessons of comfort and insight we may glean from this exquisite story.

Consider first of all, the *wonder of this woman's love for Christ*. A few deft touches from the cunning hand of this Evangelist light up for us the measure and strength of her devotion. See how pathetically she clings to all that is mortal of Christ, as if it were impossible to think of Him apart from His earthly form. "They have taken away my

Lord," she said, when what she really meant was, that some despoiler had removed His dead body. She could not picture Him apart from that form so dear to her eyes, a touch which goes straight home to all our hearts. So precious was Christ to her, that even His dead form meant more to her than all the world of living interests or human beings. See also how she lingers by the tomb, when all the others had left, as if stubbornly refusing to accept the evidence of her senses, and clinging to the pathetic delusion that some tragic blunder had been made, which would yet somehow or other come right. Notice also how her love asserted its claims even against the limitations of her physical strength. "Sir," she said, "if thou hast borne Him hence, tell me where thou hast laid Him, and I will take Him away." In her present tense mood she was prepared to measure her tiny woman's strength against the demand of supporting that heavy inert burden. Note also the recurring phrase, "my Lord," not "our Lord," as if the Lord were hers alone, as if she had proprietary rights in Him which belonged to no one else. These are exquisitely delicate touches which throw into bold relief the full rich measure of Mary's passion for Christ.

Her witness does not stand alone. Indeed it was the mark of all His followers. He was the centre of their devotion, the magnet of their hearts. He asked this love of them, and He received it. Another woman in the Gospel story (or was it the same woman?), stole into His presence at a feast, anointed His body with precious nard, kissed His feet, and wiped them, wet with her tears, with the hairs of her head. They could not help loving Him for what He was to them.

> For, Oh, the Master is so fair
> His smile so sweet to banished men,
> That they who meet Him unaware
> Can never turn to earth again.

That is intelligible, but what is really mysterious is, that that power of captivating and holding the human heart is as marked to-day as in the days of His flesh. He still grips and masters the heart of man from an unseen throne. This is the feature of the personality of Christ which puzzled and intrigued Napoleon. He himself was a leader of men and studied the rôle of influence. He knew he could extract a deathless devotion from his followers, provided he was present amongst them, galvanising them with his magnetic personal force. But Jesus had the magic power of binding men to Himself "apart from the aids of sense or sight. In defiance of time and space, the soul of man becomes an annexation to the empire of Christ. All who sincerely believe in Him experience that super-natural love towards Him. The phenomenon is quite unaccountable; it is altogether beyond the scope of man's natural powers." This devotion to the unseen Christ may be said to be the hall-mark of the Christian faith. It is what makes a man a Christian. It is also the link which binds together the whole Christian community. Peter, writing to the exiles of the Dispersion in northern Asia Minor, reminds them of the influence that binds them all together. It is Jesus, "whom having not seen ye love; in whom, though now ye see Him not, yet believing, ye rejoice with joy unspeakable and full of glory." Mary in the Garden of the Resurrection was merely the precursor of a great multitude who have spilled at the feet of Christ the treasures of their heart's devotion.

A second lesson we may learn from this incident is *the blinding power of an overmastering sorrow*. Mary's sorrow was such that she failed completely to understand the situation in which she found herself. We are constantly being told that suffering enlarges men's power of vision, and no one will deny the measure of truth in that claim. We call to mind Landor's haunting lines:

> A tear is an intellectual thing
> And a sigh is the sword of an angel king,
> And the bitter groan of the martyr's woe
> Is an arrow from the Almighty's bow.

Yet sorrow, if it be but sharp and bitter enough, dims rather than clears the vision. It draws a veil over the eyes.

It distorts the perspective. It obscures reality. It excludes from its regard vital facts that are really there—compensating and consolatory facts. Consider the obsessively blinding power of Mary's grief. It confined the object of her thoughts to our Lord's dead form. It obliterated from her memory what He Himself had said about His rising on the third day. It sealed her mind to the promises of Scripture. It made her impervious to the existence of evidence strong enough to convince Peter and John. It made her insensitive to the existence of supernatural beings at the tomb. Most serious defect of all, it prevented her from recognising her Lord, when He stood before her in the glory of His Risen life. Jesus had to speak to her twice, and with that peculiar inflection in His voice with which she was familiar, before she recognised Him. At last through her blinding grief the light broke, and, lo, the winter of her sorrow was over and gone, the ice-bound waters of her frozen heart were running free, and the time of the singing of birds had come.

This is a situation which is often repeated, and carries with it its own tragic consequences. "There is a sorrow," writes Paul, "that is unto death." Bereavement, like trial or temptation or any other of life's responsibilities, is a trust from God, and whether it confers benefit or hurt depends on our personal reactions to it. It may easily be so self-regarding and self-absorbing as to clip the wings of faith and hope. It can reduce our world to a state of blank hopelessness and despair. It can make itself proof against all the comfortable words with which human beings assail it. It can seal the mind to all the glorious promises of Scripture. Nay, it can even fail to detect the presence of the Living Christ, as He stands beside the sorrowing heart in the glory of His risen life, seeking patiently to wipe every tear from the eyes. "Why weepest thou?" Mary had some reason for her hopeless grief, as there had not yet dawned upon her closed mind the truth of the Resurrection. But it is different with us. For if we believe that Jesus died and rose again, then we ought not, on pain of sinning gravely, to "sorrow as those who have no hope."

In passing it is worth noticing, that Mary's pre-occupation with her grief for her dead master is one of the most striking evidences we possess of the truth of the Resurrection of Christ. There is a school of thinkers who assure us that there are no substantial objective proofs that such an event ever took place at all. The whole web of evidence is woven out of the threads of hysterical feelings and wishful thoughts. It was the product of over-heated imaginations. The disciples wished it to be true and so thay made it come true. The thing itself had no historical foundation or backing. It was purely a subjective illusion. Well, look at Mary, and ask yourself if her certainty was the outcome of wishful thinking. In point of fact, it was the last thing in the world she expected to happen. Her mind was hermetically sealed against the intrusion of such an idea. Her certainty came from nothing in her mental condition but from something that hap-pened to her from the outside. What convinced her was a revelation from without that forced its way through the closed shutters of her mind. It was a movement from the side of Him who was not dead but alive that overruled her stubborn incredulity, and coerced belief, in spite of herself. And that was true of all the other disciples as well. It has always seemed to me that it was the prevailing unbelief amongst all the disciple band in the possibility or at any rate the likelihood of Resurrection that constitutes the most striking proof of its historical actuality.

And now a final word *about the significance of Christ's appearance to Mary*. This personal manifestation to Mary in the Garden of the Resurrection reveals our Saviour to us in a very tender and significant light. Indeed all our Lord's relations to women in this gospel betray the most delicate sympathy with an understanding of their needs. Look at some of these instances—the distracted and em-barrassed mother at the wedding feast, the frivolous woman at the well of Jacob, the mother of sorrows at the Cross, the woman taken in adultery. Our Lord seemed to have a special solicitude for women, as if they suffered more than men, and needed His help more than others.

In the fourth Gospel He is always stretching out a helping hand to them, bringing relief to the harassed womenfolk at Cana, fountains of living water to the jaded thirsty woman at the well, protection and forgiveness to the woman of sin, life from the dead to the sorrowing sisters at Bethany, provision and security to His broken-hearted mother. Always it is a need of theirs He is meeting. Now it is a practical dilemma He meets, now a case of spiritual bankruptcy; again the burden of a scarlet sin, once more the loneliness of widowhood. And here in the Garden of the Resurrection it was a woman's hopeless ache for His presence that brought Him on swift-winged feet to her side.

There is a truth here of deathless significance. It raises and poses a question of urgent practical importance. At what place will the new revelation of death's conquest and sin's mastery break through into the world of time and sense? At what place will Christ appear to-day, and to whom, and under what circumstances? Will He go to kings, captains, leaders of men, to those occupying the seats of the mighty? To whom did He manifest Himself first after He rose from the dead? What places did He first frequent? Did He go to the Praetorium, the High priest's palace, the Sanhedrin or the Temple? It would have been natural to have done so. What a dramatic *tour de force* it would have been, if He had suddenly appeared before Pilate and said to him, "You laid Me in a tomb. You rolled a great stone to the mouth of the sepulchre. You sealed it with a Roman seal, and set a guard to watch it. Well, all your precautions have been useless. Here I am, alive." Or if He had gone to Annas and Caiaphas and said, "You despised the foundation Stone, tried and precious, that was laid in Zion. Well, the Stone which you builders had rejected is now made the Headstone of the corner." Or if He had suddenly appeared in the Temple, and said to the multitude, "You killed the heir of the vineyard, as you stoned the prophets before me. Well, here He is come back again from the dead, to claim the fruits of His vineyard." Most of us would have found it difficult to have resisted the temptation to have hoisted these crucifiers with their own petard.

But our Lord does none of these things. He is not a sensationalist. He laid that temptation low, and once for all, in the temptation in the wilderness. He is not interested in the purely dramatic. His sole concern is for human need. And the neediest person in all the world just now was a brokenhearted woman, yearning for the touch of a vanished hand and the sound of a voice that was still. This seems to me a very wonderful and significant fact. He appeared first of all to Mary, a woman who could do little to add to the kudos of His cause, whose contribution was negligible, but whose need was desperate. I say again that I know nothing more beautiful nor comforting than that.

What it means for you and me is, that we need not be afraid that we shall miss the glory of the Risen Christ, if we really want Him and need Him. If we are lonely and sad and broken-hearted, from whatever cause, and if we turn to Jesus, and seek His presence, He will come into our hearts and abide with us, and turn our sorrow into joy. If we have sinned, and gone astray in miry paths, and perhaps denied our Lord, like Peter, we shall not forfeit the gift of His presence, if we truly repent. If we are plagued with doubts, like Thomas, and find it hard to reach to any kind of spiritual certainty yet, if we seek His face with eager hope, He will make Himself known to us, and settle for us all our doubts and fears. If death has robbed us of our dearest, and we are comfortless and looking into a grey bleak future with stony hearts, like Mary, and if we but turn to Him for comfort, then the Risen Jesus on wings of mercy will speed to our aid, and with the gentle rebuke, "Why weepest thou?" He will dry the tears from our eyes, and turn our winter into spring. He will turn none away who need Him, and seek Him with all their hearts. Only to the impenitent, the adequate, the self-sufficient, and the prideful has He nothing to say. To them the heavens are empty, and swept bare of spiritual presences. But to all who supplicate His grace the Risen Christ draws near, and comforts and fortifies. As Dr. Dods puts it. "To mourn Christ's absence is to desire Him. To desire Him is to invite His presence. And to invite His presence is to secure it."

6. OUR FINAL ATTITUDE TO CHRIST
(*For decision day*)

Pilate saith unto them, What shall I do then with Jesus which is called Christ? They all say unto him, Let Him be crucified (Matt. xxvii. 22).

"What shall I do then with Jesus which is called Christ?" That question remains and will continue to remain, till it is rightly and finally settled. We cannot settle it by evading, postponing or ignoring it. We merely leave it on our hands, to emerge again in a more embarrassing form. For Jesus, the incarnate challenge of God, still confronts us, and presses for a verdict. Pilate tried to solve his problem by throwing the burden of choice on others, or allowing the drift of events to settle it for him. But it was all to no purpose. Evade it as much as he would, in the end it was he who had to choose. Pilate's question is ours also, inalienably ours. We can no more evade it now than he could then. Before we try to answer it, it is important that we should recognise its profound and far-reaching implications.

To begin with, this is a *pivotal question*.

A great deal hangs on the answer we return to it. What we do with Jesus has consequences which affect the whole area of our lives. For one thing it colours our experience of God, and settles the question whether we shall know Him merely as the transcendent Lord of Creation, the controlling force behind the universe, or whether we shall possess the assurance that He is also our Father, who cares for us and loves us with an everlasting love. It also fixes our status before God, whether He will regard us as His children accepted in His beloved Son, or look upon us as strangers to the commonwealth of grace. It settles the question whether we are children of nature, born of the flesh and of the will of man, or born again from above by the spirit of God, and heirs of everlasting life. It determines the quality of the character we now possess— its tone and strain, its tastes, appreciations, standards and values. It also shapes our life-mission and career, our dominant aims in life, the moulds into which we pour our energies, the objects we serve, the causes we support. It determines also our resources, our capacity for controlling the mutinous impulses of our nature, our adequacy to meet the tests, bear the burdens and shoulder the responsibilities of life. Someone defined an atheist as one "without invisible means of support." What we do with Jesus settles the question whether we shall meet the claims of life in our own unaided strength or have the reinforcement of a mighty invisible Ally. Last of all what we do with Jesus bears directly on our final destiny. It settles the question as to whether when death seals our mortal eyes we shall be for ever with the Lord or cast into outer darkness. This is no light trivial question that Pilate put to the Jerusalem mob, and to us. It is weighty with the burden of weal or woe for this life and that which is to come.

In the second place this *is a practical question.*

The question is not, "What shall I *say* about Jesus?" Pilate was at a loss what to say about Jesus, for he was completely puzzled by Him. His own contemporaries said the most contradictory things about Him. To some He was a bon-vivant, to others a righteous man; to some a Samaritan, to others the Messiah; to some a devil, to others the Son of God. To the rulers He was a blasphemer, a heretic and a traitor, but to Pilate He was a man in whom he could find no fault. Jesus is still the most debated and discussed Personality of history, but what men say about Him to-day as then may be interesting and have its uses, but it is outside the vital point raised by this question. Nor is the question this, "What shall I *think* about Jesus?" Right thinking about Jesus is important, for "the ancestor of every action is a thought." Our thoughts shape our belief and our belief conditions our behaviour. We ought to endeavour to think right thoughts about Jesus—the mystery of His nature, His relation to God, His work for man, His significance for human life, His unique place in God's plan of the ages. But thinking is not the same thing as doing and between the two there is often a great gulf fixed. Nor is the question this, "What shall I *feel* about Jesus?" Many people are concerned about their feelings. They test the reality of their religious experience by the strength or feebleness of their emotions. They judge their standing before God by the peace and joy that invade their lives. Feeling is not a sentiment to be despised. Love plays a large part in the Christian faith. God's gracious overture in Christ should kindle in our hearts wonder, love and praise. Yet mere emotion which is an end in itself is not enough. It ought to be an accompaniment to but never a substitute for, authentic Christian experience. It is not enough to assert our love for Christ, or deplore our lack of love, or simulate a love that is not there. The vital question is not, What shall I say or think or feel about Christ but what shall I *do*? The rich young ruler got the position right when he said to Jesus, "Good Master, what shall I *do* to inherit eternal life?" The fundamental question is neither academic nor speculative nor emotional, but severely practical. "What shall I do with Jesus? Shall I welcome Him into my life or thrust Him out of it, claim Him as my Saviour or disown Him; accept Him or reject Him, crown Him or crucify Him?" Christ comes to us as a challenge we have to meet, a decision to be made. On which side will I cast my vote, for or against Christ? "What shall I do?"

Again Pilate's question is a *present question*. It is one that has to be faced here and now. The question is not, "What have I done with Christ?" It is not, "What have I done with Him all these long days and years that are past?" Has He called me and I have not answered? Has He sought me and I have refused to be entreated? Has He come to me in word and Sacrament, in ways of Providence and grace, and have I steeled my heart against Him? Is it nothing to me that "He wept and toiled and mourned and died for love of them that loved Him not?" Have I all these years neglected His claims, betrayed the interests of His kingdom, wounded His sacred heart, turned my face from Him, and even consented to crucify Him? These are sobering reflections which may well fill our hearts with shame as we look back over the waste of the years. But Jesus, blessed be His name, does not bind the past upon us. In Him it is gloriously true, "Let the wicked forsake his way and the unrighteous man his thoughts, and let him return unto the Lord and He will have mercy upon him, and to our God, for He will abundantly pardon."

Nor does the question before us take this form, "What am I going to do with Him in the future?" Is it my intention to consider the claims of Christ only when all other claims are met and satisfied? Shall I put my pleasure and fleeting earthly interests before the demands of my soul? Shall I give to Him not my prime but my poorer baser part, not my burning enthusiasms but only the ashes of my heart? Do I regard the offer of Christ merely as a consolation prize to be accepted only when the foaming cup of life has been drained to the dregs? In this attitude to Christ there lurk two fallacies. The first concerns the nature of the Christian religion. The inference to be drawn from this procrastinating attitude is that Christ's religion is not for life at the flush but only at the ebb, an offer to be accepted as a last resort when all other resources have failed. This view is of course quite false. Jesus Christ is not a substitute for life, but life itself, its very marrow and attar. It is not meant to fit us for death, but to make life livable. The Gospel is not an ambulance device to handle casualties (although this is not excluded), but armour and equipment to meet successfully the shock of battle and fight gallantly the good fight of faith. So to all wishful to win through to victory in life's grim ordeal what we do with Jesus is a question not for the future but for the immediate demanding present. The other fallacy concerns the nature of life, that the future is ours to juggle with as we please. In point

of fact no man born of woman has any guarantee of
another hour's continuance on this planet. We hold our
tenure of life, not as a freehold but on lease, and at any
moment the lease may expire. The past is not ours
because it is lived and gone, and must be left to the
tender mercies of God. The future is all unknown and
indeed may never materialise at all. The present alone
belongs to us. "Now is the accepted time. Now is the day
of salvation." "To-day, if you will hear His voice, harden
not your hearts."

Observe again *how pressing this question is*. There are
some questions in life that can't be postponed, because of
the urgency with which they press their claims, and also
because of the menace of appalling alternatives they carry
in their heart. When the British Prime Minister flew to
Germany in 1938, he found himself faced with the
necessity for decision. He was confronted with a man
whose mind was made up, and behind him stood solidly
a mighty nation. The Führer confronted him as an active
dynamic will with a clear-cut ultimatum. To decline his
proposals or postpone their consideration to a future date
was to be faced with the appalling alternative of war. "I
must have an answer by Friday," said the Führer, "for,
if not, on Friday I will march." In such a crisis, with all
its train of consequences, to hesitate, prevaricate or postpone a decision was clearly impossible. What we shall do
with Jesus is a choice of this pressing urgency. On that
memorable day in Jerusalem, when Jesus came up for
trial before Pilate, the Roman governor was facing the
most momentous crisis of his life. The decision he had to
make was a pressing one for two reasons. The first was
that the Prisoner before him demanded a verdict. He was
there in his presence, a vital dynamic Person who made
definite claims for Himself which must be examined and
judged. They couldn't be evaded. Beyond that, however,
loomed the dark fateful consequences of a false choice.
These were the miscarriage of Roman justice, the con-
tempt of authority, the repudiation of the decencies of
life, the crucifying of Jesus, the triumph of lynch law and

mob rule. What we shall do with Jesus is a question as pressing to us as to Pilate. Jesus faces each one, not simply as an Example of holy innocence, nor as an impressive Figure of history, but as a living Contemporary the pressure of whose presence is inescapable. In a hundred ways He confronts us, beleaguering our hearts, besieging our minds, importuning our wills, intimately engaging Himself for us, with us, and in us. It is impossible for us to ignore Him or treat Him as if He were not here. Moreover He comes to us with offers and claims which He has sealed with His own blood, and which contain the alternatives of life or death. If we ignore Him or reject Him we merely open the sluice-gates of our life to the incoming tides of worldliness and sin. If we shut Him out of our lives we invite within the powers of the world, the flesh and the Devil. It is interesting to notice that the word evil is merely the word live spelt backwards. If we reject Christ, then the mechanism of the moral order runs in reverse. The dark forces of evil take control, spiritual degeneration sets in, the powers of death and darkness prevail. "How shall we escape, if we neglect so great salvation?"

Finally observe that this *is a very personal* question. "What shall *I* do with Jesus?", *not*, "What shall other people do?" Pilate tried to evade the personalness of this question. He tried to get others to solve the embarrassing problem of Jesus for him. He threw the responsibility on the shoulders of the crowd. "Let the people decide." He offered palliatives. He shamelessly and illegally scourged an innocent prisoner to gratify the mob's blood-lust, but all to no purpose. He offered them the alternative of a renegade, Barabbas, again without result. Next he tried to get Herod to conduct the trial, since Jesus was a Galilean, and failed once more. Last of all he took a basin of water, and dramatically washed his hands of the whole sordid business—a baptism unto irresponsibility. Yet in the end the choice was his, inalienably and inescapably his. History has so judged. It is an article of the Apostle's Creed that "He suffered under Pontius Pilate."

All the great choices of life are pointedly and sometimes poignantly personal. The lesser choices of life are optional. We can delegate certain things to others, the purchase of goods, furniture, clothes, details of the household menage, where we shall spend our holidays and so on. We may with advantage leave the choice of these things to our better half. There are other decisions, however, which are not optional but obligatory, such things as the choice of our friends, our partner in life, our career and such-like. And of all these decisions which each must make for himself, the most important is what we shall do with Jesus. Let us grasp the intense personalness of this question. Jesus calls us by name, speaks to us apart, and asks us separately what we are to do with Him. He presents His claims, offers us His gifts, and demands an individual response. The question of what others are saying, thinking and doing with Jesus is meantime for us irrelevant. We must make our own choice. "What shall *I* do with Jesus?" And if we hesitate we may be helped to an answer if we face this other question, "What shall I do without Jesus?" How shall I face life and its demands, death and its uncertainties, eternity and its solemn issues, if I have to face them without Jesus? Nay this question in the end is more solemnising still. For at the last the form it takes is not "What shall I do with Jesus," but "What will Jesus do with me?" Let us not forget that Jesus is the Lord of human destiny. The Father has committed all judgment to the Son. If we evade Him now and refuse to receive Him as Saviour and Lord, then to-morrow we must meet Him as our Judge, and may the Lord then have mercy on our souls. In view of all these sobering reflections, let us solemnly face the question now. "What shall I do then with Jesus, which is called Christ?" This is what I would fain persuade you to do. Kneel at His feet in humility and penitence. Yield the master key of your being to Him. Accept Him as your personal Saviour and Lord. Crown Him King and Master of your life. Consecrate all the powers of your being to His royal service. And do it with no reserve and no delay.

168

VI

EPILOGUE

THE UNAVOIDABLE CHRIST
(*For post-Easter*)

When the doors were shut where the disciples were assembled for fear of the Jews, came Jesus and stood in the midst, and said unto them, Peace be unto you (John xx. 19).

(The above sermon appeared in an abridged form in *The Expository Times* of August, 1955 and is reprinted with permission of the Editor.)

"THE doors were shut." The disciples were afraid of the Jews. They were afraid of what the authorities might do to them. They had already succeeded in disposing of their Leader. He was crucified, dead and buried. The next step was to liquidate His followers. The disciples knew that the rulers in Jerusalem were bent on putting an end once for all to this heretical and revolutionary movement, and would stop at nothing to achieve their purpose. So they were afraid for their own safety. They took the utmost precautions to avoid arrest. So they stayed indoors, went underground, locked and barred the doors of their dwelling. "The doors were shut." Every door was shut—not only the doors of their house, but the doors of their heart, the doors of their mind and will, the doors of faith and hope. "Then came Jesus, the doors being shut, and stood in the midst." Now that is very suggestive. It symbolises the truth that no barrier can ultimately shut Christ out, that no exclusion of man's devising is proof against His intrusive presence.

(1) Consider first of all how *relevant this claim is in its relation to the Jewish nation itself.* The Jewish race as a whole has always shut Christ out. They have as a matter of history locked and barred the door of their minds and hearts against Him. In the days of His flesh "He came to His own, and His own received Him not." They repudiated, spurned and scorned Him. They twisted His words,

169

distorted His teaching, disowned His claims, disputed His authority and maligned His character. They cast Him out of their synagogues, tried to stone Him to death, and in the end charged Him with blasphemy before the ecclesiastical authorities, and with treason at the bar of Caesar. They succeeded in working their will upon Him, and suspending Him on a Cross like a common criminal.

But they have not succeeded in getting rid of Him. Cast out with shame and contumely He is coming back again. The folly of His rejection haunts them like a nemesis. The Figure of Jesus, like a black shadow, rests heavily on the soul of modern Jewry. His majestic Personality teases and torments their mind and conscience. They can't help thinking about Him. Their finest minds are drawn to Him, and some of the best of modern books on Jesus are written by Jews. Many of them are beginning to wonder if their race has not committed a tragic and fatal blunder. Not a few are hailing Him as the bright and morning Star of their Messianic hopes. The statistics for Jewish missions are amongst the most hopeful and promising in the records of modern missionary enterprise. And there is a day coming, God speed the day, when not only the fulness of the Gentiles but the outcasts of Israel shall be gathered within the fold of the Good Shepherd.

(2) Consider again *how impossibly difficult it is for us moderns to escape His influence*. We may refuse to recognise His claim on our lives. We may reject His ethics and disbelieve His doctrine. We may refuse to recognise His right to control and mould our being. We may try to ignore His very existence, and treat Him as if He had never died and rises again for us men and our salvation, as many are attempting to do. But when every door is shut He still stands in the midst. For one thing He meets us along every road of life we travel. There is not a single typical human experience in which He is not implicated. When we present our children for baptism it is in His name they are baptised. When we stand at the marriage altar husbands and wives are commanded to love one another as Christ loved the Church. The last low whispers of our

dead are burdened with His name. As we commit them to their last resting place it is with His great words ringing in our ears, "I am the Resurrection and the Life." And when death seals our mortal eyes it is but to open them to the vision of the resplendent Christ no man can avoid. But it is not only in the great experience of life that Christ is inevitable but in its normal processes. Christ has so woven Himself into the warp and woof of our normal ways of living that we cannot escape Him. Every time a business man sits down to write a letter He dates it from Christ's birth at Bethlehem. One day in seven is called the Lord's Day, and is set apart for the worship of His name. Every book we read that has enduring value is deeply tinctured with His mind. Every Church in every village is an eloquent reminder of His claims upon us. Every noble Christian life we see is an epistle of Christ read and known of all men. And every Christian institution in our land that enriches social life is stamped with the hallmark of His presence. The very sound waves that fill the air whisper His blessed name in our ears. Shut Him out as we may, He still stands in the midst.

(3) Consider *once again how true this is whenever we picture to ourselves what the good life means, and how it ought to be lived.* Jesus Himself is the ground work and pattern of morality. "Talk they of morality, O thou bleeding Lamb, the true morality is love of Thee." Jesus Himself is the gold standard of the moral currency of the human race. It is by His flawless excellence we test the worth of our morality. As Samuel Butler wrote, "He publishes anew the laws of our character, which men had corrupted, the very existence of which to a large extent had been forgotten." The four absolute standards of love, honesty, purity and unselfishness are merely academic words apart from Christ. It is He who gives them flesh and blood. It is only when we come face to face with Jesus that we know what the good life is like.

And when we try to live it He becomes even more inevitable. We need His all-availing help in our moral struggles. And it is our experience that in point of fact we

receive it. We may not consciously seek His aid. We may
reply on ourselves alone, on the exercise of our will-power,
on self-discipline, self-control and the like, yet it remains
true that the moment we try to climb upwards, Jesus
Himself draws near us, and strengthens us with might by
His Spirit in the inner man of the heart.

This also must be said. Even when we fall from the good
life, break our vows, betray the Christ in us, fall into
shameful and degrading sins, we are once more face to
face with the inevitable Christ. For His is a love that never
lets us go. He follows us into every far country of spiritual
forsakenness, and even if we make our bed in Hell He is
there also. We may well despair of our own moral
recovery; our friends may wash their hands of us; even
the Church may lose its interest in us; but there is One
who never leaves us nor forsakes us. By the compunctions
of conscience, by the burning fires of remorse, by the
wretchedness of frustration which our sin produces in us,
He signalises His presence. The familiar legend, known as
"Quo vadis?" tells how Peter denied His Lord a second
time. Peter was in Rome, in danger of his life, so he sought
safety in flight. As he sped along the Campagna, he was
met by a vision of the risen Christ travelling in the
direction of Rome.

> Lo, on the darkness brake a wandering ray,
> A vision flashed along the Appian way;
> Divinely on the pagan night it shone,
> A mournful Face, a Figure hurrying on;
> Though haggard and dishevelled, frail and worn,
> A king of David's lineage, crowned with thorn.
> "Lord, whither farest?" Peter wondering cried.
> "To Rome," said Christ, "to be recrucified."
> Into the night the vision ebbed like breath,
> And Peter turned and rushed on Rome and death.

That may be legend, but this at least is true, that the
darker the betrayal, the more solicitous His concern, and
the farther we wander from Him, the closer we are pur-
sued by His seeking, saving love.

Consider finally another facet of this subject. *When we try to help others we find ourselves face to face with the unavoidable Christ.* When our motive for service is the constraint of Christ's own love, it is not surprising that He should take up His abode in our hearts. But what is unexpected is that the same result should take place when that service is rendered without regard to His will and purpose. There are multitudes of uncanonised benefactors in our midst. There are men and women in every rank and class who, in obedience to the kindly impulses of their nature, seek to undo heavy burdens and let the oppressed go free. They do not name the name of Christ. His concern for the welfare of men is not in any of their thoughts. Their motive for service has its source in human compassion and pity alone. Nevertheless, in doing what they do, they find Christ's spirit of compassion brooding in their hearts. As they try to comfort others the Comforter divine draws near. As they seek to counsel those distracted by perplexity, the Holy Spirit of Truth dwells within them and guides into all truth. As they try to break the fetters of vice which grip with iron bands the soul of a lost brother, the great Emancipator becomes their Ally and sheds on them the smile of His approval. The Friend of friends draws near to us in the friends we befriend.

> Hush, I pray you?
> What if the friend happens to be—God.

This is true even of atheistic service, if for the moment we may speak of such a thing. It is quite possible formally to exclude from our service of others all the sanctions of the Christian faith, turn our backs on Christ and act altruistically on the basis of a godless creed. Yet, spite of our blindness and prejudice, if we yet act selflessly and hold to our purpose of advancing the good of our fellows, He will stand in the midst, and whisper to our hearts, "Inasmuch as ye have done it unto the least of these, my brethren, have ye done it unto Me." The red Dean of Canterbury some time ago visited Russia to investigate for himself the results of the new social experiment of

Communism. As a Christian he was particularly anxious that the Church should have some share in this new social planning. He therefore ventured to put in a good word for Christ. His Russian friends refused to listen to his suggestion. They scoffed at the idea of reintroducing into their scheme of things this out-worn superstitition. But as the Dean listened in greater detail to an exposition of their blue-print for education and their schemes of social reconstruction, he was constrained to exclaim, "Why, but all this is but the Sermon on the Mount brought up to date." "The doors, being shut, Jesus stood in the midst."

Or look again at the problem of peace, the very gift Christ offers in this connection. Peace is what everyone wants and needs and which no one seems able to make or get. Peace in the modern world is as elusive as a will-o'-the-wisp, or the receding mirage in the desert. Have you ever thought that the real obstacle to peace is men's rejection of the claims of Christ? The heads of nations meet regularly in solemn conclave, and engage in wordy combat. One Person, however, is excluded from the Council chamber. His will is not consulted. His help is not asked. No prayers are offered to Him for guidance and direction. His writ does not run in their assemblies. And no progress is ever made. Frustration and futility attend all their efforts. One day when our pooled corporate wisdom is seen to be what it is, foolishness, and the nations begin to consider, not their own selfish national interests but the general good of mankind, then, even if they do not name the name of Christ, even if every door is locked against Him, through every closed door He will pass, and stand in the midst and speak peace to His people. God speed the day!

But why should we seek to evade Him whom yet we cannot evade? A certain Hyde Park orator was recently addressing a large crowd of people on the demerits of the Christian faith. He was particularly vitriolic against Christ—debunking His claims, deriding His doctrine, discrediting His character and even denying His very existence. At the close a woman in the crowd asked this devastating question. "If He is the nonentity you make Him out to be, why can't you leave Him alone?" We leave other people alone, even the illustrious dead, who "from their storied urns" no longer disturb us. We leave them alone, because they leave us alone. But that is precisely the one thing Jesus never does. "He besets us behind and before and lays His hand upon us." We can't leave Him alone, because He refuses to leave us alone. He passes through every closed door of our hearts, through all our prejudices, suspicions, hesitations and unbelief, and stands in the midst. He disturbs our conscience, beleaguers our hearts and besieges our will. And He whispers peace to our troubles. Why try to evade Him who so solicitously seeks us? Is He not the adored and altogether adorable One? Is He not the bearer of all life's moral and spiritual values? Is He not the Light of all our seeing, the Life of all our living, and the end of all life's quests? Shall we not rather run to Him for shelter and adventure, for power and peace, for salvation from sin and the final judgment, and sanctify Him as Lord in our hearts?